Putting Your Words to Work

Learn to Use the Voice of Authority

by
Lance Ivey

Tulsa, OK

Table of Contents

Foreword

In various respects, the church has lost its voice. I didn't say we've lost our ministry or our ability to speak. I say we've lost our voice, and it's not that we are not saying anything. It's more like, "Do we have something to say?" The distinction is found in why they said of Jesus, "He teaches as one who has authority."

This is why Lance Ivey has written a very important book for such a time as this. Putting Your Words To Work is a guideline to lead the church back to its rightful place of authority in the use of our words. In certain corridors of the church we have artfully shared the importance of confessing the Word and not the circumstances we're facing, but we don't tell people how to do it, and we have rendered the process fruitless, and to a large degree, without authority. In this pivotal book and important work, Lance not only defines and clarifies significant truths about speaking the word of God with authority, but he also shows with simplicity and practicality how to put our everyday words to work.

What secularists call self-talk and we call confession is valuable and essential to a fully productive life. Psycholinguistics is a study that tells us how our words affect our lives. It is the secular version for what we call the biblical doctrine of confession. It has been proven that if you confess something it gets into your personal belief system 10%.

If you confess it with imagination, it gets into your belief system 55%. If you confess it with imagination and emotion it gets into your belief system 100%. You can then confess something with the authority to change your circumstances and your life. In faith you learn to confess something in a personal way, in present tense statements and with positive declarations. The result is authority to change your life.

Lance Ivey has always been a great thinker and communicator. He has now penned a tool to help you and the church to reclaim its place on the planet and to garner the unlimited power of the Kingdom of God.

Ron McIntosh

President, Ron McIntosh Ministries

www.ronmcintoshministries.com

Executive Director, Victory Bible College

Director of Education, Victory Christian School

Tulsa, OK

Author of *Keep the Flame Burning, The Quest for Revival, The Greatest Secret* & *Organic Christianity*

What Others are Saying

"This amazing resource by Lance Ivey is not just a book, it's a compelling experience and life-impacting journey. Each chapter that you read opens the eyes of your understanding and challenges you to dig deeper in the Word of God . As you read through Putting Your Words To Work, you'll find it's stacked up so beautifully and thoroughly that it feels more like a clearly written out playbook and he is the coach. "Coach" Lance is an amazing teacher, speaker, and encourager. I know this life-changing book will bless you the way it has blessed me. It serves like a great playbook, and as a good coach will tell you, "if you run the play" you can get the results you desire."

Pastor Skip Henderson

World Outreach Center, Milwaukee, WI

"Lance Ivey has, with faithful passion, pressed into the Lord seeking wisdom, revelation, understanding and knowledge on releasing the authority entrusted to the Body of Christ. The Lord's response, penned by Lance's obedient ear, speaks through the pages of this book. I personally purchased, "Putting Your Words To Work" for those leading ministries in the church for which I pastor, and has proven to be a very fruitful investment."

John Short Jr
Founding Pastor, Maine Life Gate Church
Limerick, ME

"I've seen Lance's life and what he's overcome through speaking with Authority into impossible situations, and to be honest...I'm stunned by the results. This book slams the door on the errors, excesses and immature understanding of faith and confession, and uncovers relational and true biblical authority through our words again to a new generation of Joshua's facing their Jericho's."

Jeff Baldwin

Lead Pastor, The Refuge Church DFW

Bedford, TX

Introduction: First Words

Whenever we set out on a journey or pursue completion of a project, one of the most important things we first must do is to set expectations and goals. In that process, we must choose words that accurately reflect and express what it is we want prioritized and accomplished. We do well to write the expectations and goals we desire with specifically chosen words. And then, we must understand and use our voice—the voice of authority given to us by God—with the stated intention of knowing how to use biblical confession as spiritual law to create, establish, and fully experience the life God has always intended for us to live—in short, to transform our lives from where we are to where we desire to be as a daily living reality.

Much has been made of the topic of words and man's capacity to speak. A person eloquent in speech has been described as having a tongue that works like the pen of a ready writer. Man has been described as a thinking and "speaking spirit" created in the image and likeness of God to function in the earth in god-like manner. Social philosophers of earlier centuries proclaimed the belief that the "pen is mightier than the sword," emphasizing that rightly chosen words carry force and power that exceeds that of raw might and violence.

What is it about words, both written and spoken, that cause such explosive, dynamic, and effective power to be lodged within them? No matter what other qualities we may attribute to the power in the words we voice, the character, integrity, and authority behind those words are definitive keys that reveal the source of this power. And most notably, the authority that backs spoken words is at the heart of why speaking with the voice of authority can be so potent.

Matthew 7:29 describes the impression Jesus left on people after hearing Him speak: "And so it was, when Jesus had ended these sayings, that the people were astonished at His teaching, for He taught them as one having authority, and not as the scribes."

Luke presented the same observation after Jesus taught the Word of God to the crowds that populated His gatherings. Luke 4:32 says, "And they were astonished at His teaching, for His word was with authority." After using His words to minister to a man to expel a "spirit of an unclean demon," the people who witnessed this "were all amazed and spoke among themselves, saying, What a word this is! For with authority and power He commands the unclean spirits, and they come out." (Luke 4:36)

In these instances, Jesus was demonstrating and releasing the voice of authority in the earth. When the voice of authority was used, things around Him changed to conform to the directions He spoke.

The same things spoken about Jesus as He used the voice of authority should be spoken about every believer. I know how seemingly unrealistic that sounds but if any part of the Body of Christ speaks with His authority, they are entitled to the same results that Jesus experienced in His body while He was in the earth.

With that in mind, the words presented here are offered as a concise resource to describe and define the voice of authority and to teach us how to grow in our understanding, expertise and use of the voice of authority. The intent is that you will obtain added substance to build convictions and instill staying power through scriptural truth that endures to all generations. The serving element of this resource is to feed your spirit, fortify your soul and offer nourishment that lends itself to developing an ever increasingly prosperous soul. The living element is designed for you to experience the productive fruit of speaking with the voice of authority in such a way that the quality of your life and the lives of those around you, are verifiably made better.

If you want something that works for a lifetime, you will find proven things that work in these pages, but it may take some time and effort to experience the fullest results. Yet rest assured that once truth is settled in place in your heart, it will produce a steady stream of right results. Jesus made this kind of guarantee in John 8:31-32 where it's recorded, "If you continue in My word, you are My disciples indeed. And you shall know the truth, and the truth shall make you free." The effort you invest from this day forward in speaking with the voice of authority will be well worth your time, both for a lifetime in the earth and beyond.

Chapter 1
The Ancient Art of Confession

The ancient art of confession has its basis in the voice of authority. Biblical confession, or proper use of right words based on scriptural truth, is a biblical principle and spiritual reality rooted in God, and it is ingrained in the fabric of His very nature. We find the earliest evidence of the voice of authority in the Bible describing the period of time called "in the beginning."

The book of Genesis gives an accurate account of what God said with authority to direct the physical world into the structure and shape of His intentions and instructions. In the Genesis 1 account, God repeatedly spoke what He desired and believed, and He saw the concrete results of what He spoke.

As we see from Isaiah 46:10-11, God speaks His intended outcomes from the beginning of His plans. The voice of authority is instrumental in the process of bringing "things" to pass.

Declaring the end from the beginning, and from ancient times things that are not yet done, saying, My counsel shall stand, and I will do all my pleasure.

Indeed, I have spoken it, I will also bring it to pass; I have purposed it, I will also do it.

Isaiah 46:10-11b NKJV

God has employed this method of *"declaring the end from the beginning"* in every aspect of His kingdom. God has determined from ancient times that things He wants to come into existence will be voiced from His originating authority. And what He speaks He will bring it to pass and do it. Confession isn't merely something God does, it's contained within the nature of who He is, how He lives and the purpose behind why He does things the way He does. Confession is defined within the measure of His self-existent nature.

It's so important to see and understand that confession isn't just a principle men have discovered over the past 50 or 100 years. Although confession can help facilitate the acquisition of financial and material provision, it's not a toy for purely personal enjoyment. Confession isn't a weapon to attack people we dislike, nor is it a part of an arsenal for the arrogant to wield. Confession has deeper purposes. Consider these five points that illustrate the long standing significance of confession.

First, confession is an ancient kingdom reality and divine law that's rooted in God. God used the release of words in confession to create the heavens and the earth, and to speak the physical universe and the realm of time into existence.

Second, this process of spoken words is what Satan attempted to use to usurp authority and overthrow God in an attempt to undermine the entire corporate structure of heaven and the Kingdom of God. Satan attempted to take over ruling power in the Kingdom of God, but God easily and clearly demonstrated His superiority over His created subordinate. God exerted and imposed an effective defense, a steadfast resistance, and an overwhelming offensive assault against Satan through what He spoke against the enemy.

Third, confession was involved in what Jesus strategically employed to authorize His resurrection so as to fulfill the plan of redemption and preserve the human race as the family of God. The actions that corresponded with what Jesus said were of obvious importance, but the alignment of His heart with His words was required to succeed in the work.

Fourth, biblical confession is what a person is authorized to use for experiencing the new birth, to be born again. There is a day coming where every knee will bow and every tongue shall confess that Jesus Christ is Lord to the glory of God. The wise person chooses by the power and action of their will to do so now in this life here in the earth rather than later in the judgment that follows physical death.

And fifth, because of the reality of eternal life, the re-born child of God is to aggressively, intentionally, and proactively use this divine law of confession to help them mature into the fullness of this new nature freely given by God. This includes, but is not limited to, the training of the spirit to speak with the voice of authority for material provisions, healing and health, a successful vocational career and ministry, sound and fulfilling relationships, good reputation and overall respectability, excellence and well-being in life.

Let's look at each of these five areas listed above more closely.

Five Basic Truths You Must Understand About Biblical Confession

TRUTH #1: Confession is an ancient kingdom reality and divine law that's rooted in God.

God used the release of words in confession to create the heavens and the earth, and to speak the physical universe and the realm of time into existence.

> *By faith we understand that the worlds were framed by the word of God, so that things which are seen were not made of things which are visible.*
>
> *Hebrews 11:3 NKJV*

Many times this verse is used in connection to the Creation account in Genesis 1, but the literal context of this verse in Hebrews 11 is strongly inclusive of and dealing with periods of time and not singularly with the physical worlds. But the principle still applies significantly to the physical creation. Let's study this through.

I recognize noted Greek scholar Rick Renner for helping me to understand several of the words and concepts surrounding the first few verses of Hebrews 11 in much better light. As stated by Mr. Renner, "if Hebrews 11:3 was referring specifically to creation, one of two Greek words would have been used, either the Greek word kosmos or oikoumene (oy-kou-men-ay) would have been written. Kosmos refers to the universe. Oikoumene refers to the physical planet earth or to the inhabited parts of the earth. Most likely, had the writer of Hebrews been talking primarily about the creation account, he would have used *kosmos* or *oikoumene*, but neither one of these words was used here."

Instead the Greek word used here is the word *aion*. *Aion* describes specific periods of time in the history of man, like a year, a decade, a century, or millennium. This specific period of time has a concrete beginning, and it has a concrete ending. An *aion* would be a specific, allotted period of time, again anywhere from a day or less, or up to a millennium or more. You can measure an allotted time from its beginning to its end—it has a very specific beginning and a very specific ending that can be demonstrated, measured, and proven.

This could also describe a generation, because a generation has a beginning and an ending. It certainly would apply to the Creation account. God began "in the beginning" and rested from His work after six days. He completed or ended His work after a specific period of time.

Hebrews 11:3 could be translated, "Through faith we understand, that different time periods, different generations within the history of mankind were framed—created and established—by the Word of God."

Let's also consider here the word used for "framed." It's the Greek word katartizō and means "to render fit, sound and complete; to mend or repair something broken; to arrange, adjust and put in order; to restore and strengthen and to make one what he ought to be." It also means "to take something already existing and to re-fashion it or to completely reshape it."

Again, the principle is sound in that God made the earth fit, sound and complete—so the impact of what God said in the physical Creation process is demonstrated. Remember how Genesis 1:2 says *"the earth was without form, and void and darkness was on the face of the deep?"* The earth came into a place of being arranged, adjusted, and put in order. The earth was in existence but somehow came to be without form, void and dark. God took something already existing and re-fashioned it and reshaped the visible appearance so that it was re-ordered through light to take the shape of His desire.

When did this happen? According to Genesis 1:1, this happened in the beginning.

How long did this take place? Genesis 1 gives a measure of six days. Genesis 2:1-2 says God rested on the seventh day—not because He was exhausted and in no shape to continue, but because He had completed His work. The job was done.

How did this happen? God said. He spoke to create and fashion the world in which man was to live. Look at how many times we see a reference to God speaking in Genesis 1.

Then God said, "Let there be light: and there was light." Then God said, "Let there be a firmament..." And God called the firmament Heaven. Then God said, "Let the waters under the heaven be gathered together unto one place, and let the dry land appear..." And God called the dry land Earth... Then God said, "Let the Earth bring forth grass, the herb that yields seed, and the fruit tree that yields fruit according to its kind, whose seed is in itself, on the earth..." Then God said, Let there be lights in the firmament of the heavens..." Then God said, "Let the earth bring forth the living creature according to its kind..." Then God said, "Let Us make man in Our image, according to Our likeness: and let them have dominion over..." Then God blessed them, and God said to them, "Be fruitful and multiply; fill (replenish) the earth, and subdue it: and have dominion over..."

Genesis 1:3, 6, 8-11, 14, 24, 26, 28 NKJV

These statements are not just recorded in the Bible for

the purpose of having an historical account of what was said. This verbal process is highlighted to reveal key components in the creative process. What happened when "God said" these words? God saw what He said come to pass. Genesis 1:31 says, "Then God saw everything that He had made, and indeed it was very good." If you go back and look at it, in each case found in Genesis 1 where "God said," you'll find these confirming statements: "and it was so," and "God saw that it was good."

There are a few important points to make about this pattern of operation God employs.

God doesn't panic in the process of making things the way He wants them to be.

God uses words to change what's seen.

Things were so when God said it was so, not when He saw it was so.

When we say what He said we can see what is meant to be so.

We can see what's good when we say what He said.

Words are designed to create, see and experience what's good in the sight of God.

Words are primarily to be used for the creation of worlds in which to live.

Every world has an atmosphere. Some atmospheres are easier to live in than others. At certain times and seasons, the temperatures in certain parts of the world rise and fall to uncomfortable levels. Without climate control equipment and technology or without proper shelter and clothing, those conditions can become unbearable, even deadly. When we use our words skillfully, we can engage in a measure of personal climate control and create better worlds, better atmospheres in which to live, raise our families, work and serve God. Things we say come to pass when we base and maintain what we say on what He said.

Why did it all come to pass in Genesis exactly like He said? He had the authority to bring these things He said into existence. *Why does He have this authority?* God has this authority through the supremacy of self-existence and by rights of ownership through creation. He doesn't require the assistance, aid, permission, or help of anyone or anything to exist and continue in existing, to function and keep on functioning, to live and go on living, to be powerful and perpetually persist in being powerful. He originated the creation so He retains full rights, authorities, and privileges over His Creation. Consequently, He can delegate that authority and its use to whomever He wills.

Notice how many times the word "said" or "called" appears. How does this relate to us in the here and now? Think about it. We're designed and built in the image and likeness of God, and if we're born again and have spirits recreated in His nature, we are given the rights of sons and daughters—the authority that comes with being the offspring of God. John 1:12-13 proves this out even further.

> *But as many as received Him, to them He gave the right to become children of God, to those who believe in His name: Who were born, not of blood, nor of the will of the flesh, nor of the will of man, but of God.*

> *John 1:12-13 NKJV*

Being God's children and crafted with His DNA, we have inherent qualities and characteristics in like manner as our Divine Parent. John 4:24 says, *"God is a Spirit."* Genesis 1 clearly reveals that God speaks. If God is a speaking spirit, then it stands to reason that His offspring take on the same nature as He possesses. This means that any man, woman or child who has become a part of God's family is also a speaking spirit after His image and likeness. The world, and those outside the family of God, speak from one frame of reference and a different source of authority than the offspring of God. The principle of being a spirit being that speaks can still work for the person in the world but from a different spiritual source, from a different authority and motivation.

As speaking spirits in the family of God, what we say orders the events of our lives and builds the way things begin to come to pass from a supernatural, divine, kingdom of God perspective. When we have authority, resources, personnel and a plan that all come from God, what we say takes on clear focus and shape. Our saying directs our way. Our saying clears the way for what we believe, imagine and speak to be manufactured before our eyes and come to pass in our daily lives. Over time, our daily lives become the sum total of the body of words we consistently speak. Just like God.

TRUTH #2: This process of spoken words is what Satan attempted to use to usurp authority and overthrow God in an attempt to undermine the entire corporate structure of heaven and the Kingdom of God.

Satan attempted to take over ruling power in the Kingdom of God, but God easily and clearly demonstrated His superiority over His created subordinate. God exerted and imposed an effective defense, a steadfast resistance and an overwhelming offensive assault against Satan through what He spoke against the enemy.

Satan—or as he is referred to in Isaiah 14, Lucifer—saw the success of God's confessions and thought to use God's way of doing things to take over the leadership in heaven. He sought to say and do what he saw his Creator do. As applied here in Isaiah 14, confession is "a declaration to release and enforce one's will." Notice what Lucifer said in his heart as the expression of his contradictory will.

For you have said in your heart: 'I will ascend into heaven, I will exalt my throne above the stars of God;

I will also sit on the mount of the congregation on the farthest sides of the north; I will ascend above the heights of the clouds, I will be like the Most High.

Isaiah 14:13-14 NKJV

What did God have to say about this? What was God's original perspective of Satan's words and devices?

How you are fallen from heaven, O Lucifer, son of the morning! How you are cut down to the ground, you who weakened the nations!

Isaiah 14:12 NKJV

Lucifer sought to use the authority enforced and reality building statement, "I will," but neglected to use it in respect to God ordained authority. God responded from His place of legal rights, primary power, and overriding authority as creator of all things, and put Lucifer in his proper place.

Yet you shall be brought down to Sheol (hell), to the lowest depths of the Pit.

Isaiah 14:15 NKJV

Notice what God said about Lucifer's attempts to overthrow heaven in Ezekiel 28.

You were the anointed cherub who covers; and I established (set) you: you were on the holy mountain

*of God; you walked back and forth in the midst of fiery
stones.*

Ezekiel 28:14 NKJV

God had initially given Lucifer an exalted place in
His presence as His will for Lucifer. God set him and
established him in his appointed place. It was his God
ordained or authorized place. It was in the place God set
Lucifer—here in this place and here only—where Lucifer
had an established right from which to speak and confess
the intents of his will.

*Therefore thus saith the Lord God; because thou hast
set thine heart as the heart of God...*

Ezekiel 28:6 KJV

With his words, Satan expressed his will and set his heart
in a place in which he wasn't ordained or, in other words, he
wasn't authorized. The anointed cherub attempted to take
over God's place and God didn't set his heart or his rights
there. Lucifer set his own course apart from God's will. He
only endeavored to mimic God in a formula and principle,
but detached himself from the spirit and nature that ignited
the authority to speak transformational words.

Notice the result of confessing apart from God's expressed
will as understood through God's spoken or written word.

You were perfect in your ways from the day you were created till iniquity was found in you. "By the abundance of your trading you became filled with violence within, and you sinned; therefore I cast you as a profane thing out of the mountain of God; and I destroyed you, O covering cherub, from the midst of the fiery stones. "Your heart was lifted up because of your beauty; you corrupted your wisdom for the sake of your splendor; I cast you to the ground, I laid you before kings, that they might gaze at you. "You defiled your sanctuaries by the multitude of your iniquities, by the iniquity of your trading; therefore I brought fire from your midst; it devoured you, and I turned you to ashes upon the earth in the sight of all who saw you. All who knew you among the peoples are astonished at you; you have become a horror, and shall be no more forever."

Ezekiel 28:15-19 NKJV

Confession also means "saying the same things as." Lucifer obviously determined in his heart and from a stance of pride to say things that were different from God's heart and will. Lucifer spoke things that opposed God. Saying the same things as God—from a heart in sync with God's word, nature, and will—is one of the most important keys to right confession, particularly in using the voice of authority.

In Hebrews 3:1, Jesus is called the High Priest and Apostle of our profession or confession. Christianity itself is called the Great Confession. That's why Hebrews 10:23 says, "Let us hold fast the profession of our faith without wavering..." It's made clear that we are to hold fast to saying the same things as God said in relation to our faith, and to do so with a steadfast and unwavering resolve.

In the operation of authority, it's important to remember that God only backs what He wills. The best practice is to find out God's will to know what must be confessed for your life and in the earth. Saying the same things as God says is of the utmost importance. And within that, a key issue isn't only saying the same things as God says, but also having a heart that is in alignment or in deep agreement and unity with what God says. It's true that a person can "school" themselves into this place, but the truth remains that results take place when the heart is aligned in word and belief with what God says. This is when the voice of authority is most effective.

TRUTH #3: Confession was involved in what Jesus strategically employed to authorize His resurrection so as to fulfill the plan of redemption and preserve the human race as the family of God.

The actions that corresponded with what Jesus said were of obvious importance, but the alignment of His heart with His words was required to succeed in the work.

While the disciples were ignorant of why Jesus said what

He did about His future, Jesus himself had a keen awareness of the impact of His words on His mission, and His will on His words. Matthew's gospel gives four individual accounts on what Jesus said in relation to the days He was about to face on the way to and through the cross. In connection to His resurrection, Jesus spoke with authority about things to come.

Now as they came down from the mountain, Jesus commanded them, saying, "Tell the vision to no one until the Son of Man is risen from the dead."

Matthew 17:9 NKJV

Now while they were staying in Galilee, Jesus said to them, "The Son of Man is about to be betrayed into the hands of men, And they will kill Him, and the third day He will be raised up." And they were exceedingly sorrowful.

Matthew 17:22-23 NKJV

"Behold, we are going up to Jerusalem, and the Son of Man will be betrayed to the chief priests and to the scribes; and they will condemn Him to death, And deliver Him to the Gentiles to mock and to scourge and to crucify. And the third day He will rise again."

Matthew 20:18-19 NKJV

Then Jesus said to them, "All of you will be made to stumble because of Me this night, for it is written: 'I will strike the Shepherd, and the sheep of the flock will be scattered.' But after I have been raised, I will go before you to Galilee."He went a little farther and fell on His face, and prayed, saying, "O My Father, if it is possible, let this cup pass from Me; nevertheless, not as I will, but as You will." So he left them, went away again, and prayed the third time, saying the same words.

Matthew 26:31-32, 39, 44 NKJV

Notice that on four separate occasions, Jesus spoke the same words about His resurrection. In voicing these statements, Jesus was doing at least five things:

1. *He was aligning His heart and words with the prophetic declarations established by God and written in the scriptures.*

2. *He was expressing His faith and trust in the written word of God.*

3. *He was releasing the voice of authority inherent in His God ordained place.*

4. *He was giving permission and authorizing His participation in the plan, purpose, and will of God for His life in the earth.*

5. *He was confessing the words necessary to set in motion spiritual laws and principles, the spiritual machinery and spiritual operations to produce tangible results and bring into appearance the things He spoke.*

Where did Jesus get the raw material and spiritual knowledge to generate both the confession and reality of His resurrection? He got it directly from three places: from the scriptures, from an inspired conversation and endorsement, and from a command given by God.

Jesus' voice of authority for resurrection was empowered by scriptures like Psalm 16:10-11, "For you will not leave My soul in Hell, nor will you allow Your Holy One to see corruption. You will show me the path of life." His voice was also empowered by Isaiah 53:10-12, "Yet it pleased the Lord to bruise Him; He has put Him to grief. When You make His soul an offering for sin, He shall see His seed, He shall prolong His days, and the pleasure of the Lord shall prosper in His hand. He shall see the labor of His soul, and be satisfied. By His knowledge My righteous Servant shall justify many, for He shall bear their iniquities. Therefore I will divide Him a portion with the great, and He shall divide the spoil with the strong, because He poured out His soul unto death..."

Jesus also drew inspired authority to voice what He did about His resurrection from the conversation He had on the Mount of Transfiguration with Moses and Elijah. Luke 9:31 says they "spoke of His decease which He was about to accomplish at Jerusalem." During the conversation, Peter thought to pay homage to Jesus, Moses and Elijah and build altars of worship to acknowledge each of them equally. God broke in to say, "This is My beloved Son, in whom I am well

26

The Ancient Art of Confession

pleased. Hear Him." In other words, God was saying that Jesus is the one with authority to speak above Moses and Elijah. What He says will stand and come to pass.

In Matthew 17:9, Jesus told the disciples who heard the conversations to say nothing of it "until the Son of Man is risen from the dead." Moses, Elijah and Jesus spoke of His death, and it would appear from what Jesus says here, they also spoke of His resurrection. By declaring, "Hear Him," God placed a spiritual endorsement on what Jesus said and authorized Jesus to speak of His resurrection with absolute certainty.

Perhaps the greatest evidence of what upheld Jesus' voice of authority is the testimony given by Jesus Himself of the personal assurance given to Him by His Father.

Therefore My Father loves Me, because I lay down My life that I may take it again. No one takes it from Me, but I lay it down of Myself. I have power to lay it down, and I have power to take it again. This command I have received from My Father.

John 10:17-18 NKJV

What a powerful and revealing insight to the voice of authority. The same principles behind why Jesus could use the voice He had with such authority are true for us. What has God commanded upon your life, into your life and through your life? This is what you have authority to voice

and expect with confidence to come to pass.

Jesus came into alignment in heart and word with these things; He came to know about Himself from the written Word, from a divinely inspired meeting and from the personal word of command He heard spoken by His Father. When we use the voice of authority this way, the same alignment in heart and word is to be seen in us, and we will produce greater and greater results from what we say.

TRUTH #4: Biblical confession is what a person is authorized to use for experiencing the new birth, to be born again.

There is a day where every knee will bow and every tongue shall confess that Jesus Christ is Lord to the glory of God. The wise person chooses by power and act of their will to do so now in this life here in the earth rather than later in the judgment that follows death.

Remember, John 1:12 says, "But as many as received Him (Jesus) to them He gave the rights to become children of God, to those who believe in His name." We receive Him in belief, word and deeds of the heart. Paul wrote in Romans 10 the simplicity of how we accept Jesus as Lord: Believe in the heart that God has raised Jesus from the dead and confess with the mouth the Lord Jesus. This speaks of alignment with what God has said of Jesus. "He is the Way, the Truth and the Life." This also speaks of alignment with what Jesus said of Himself: "No man comes to the Father except through the Son. I am the resurrection and the life. He who believes in Me, though he may die, he shall live."

Let's look for a few moments at the full context of what Paul wrote in Romans 10 on how to receive eternal life—the place of right standing with God through faith and the role the voice of authority plays in being born again to newness of life.

> *But the righteousness of faith speaks in this way, "Do not say in your heart, 'Who will ascend into heaven?'" (that is, to bring Christ down from above or, "'Who will descend into the abyss?'" (that is, to bring Christ up from the dead). But what does it say? "The word is near you, in your mouth and in your heart" (that is, the word of faith which we preach): That if you confess with your mouth the Lord Jesus and believe in your heart that God has raised Him from the dead, you will be saved. For with the heart one believes unto righteousness, and with the mouth confession is made unto salvation. For the Scripture says, "Whoever believes on Him will not be put to shame." For there is no distinction between Jew and Greek, for the same Lord over all is rich to all who call upon Him. For "whoever calls on the name of the Lord shall be saved."*
>
> *Romans 10:6-13 NKJV*

Being saved, receiving eternal life, being born again—however we describe it—is saying that we have a good and right standing with God, or righteousness. There is no righteousness with God apart from faith. We know that faith comes by hearing the Word of God. We also know that faith is released by speaking and acting on the Word of God.

The first place of faith being released is when a person recognizes God for who He is, and acknowledges Jesus for who He is as Lord. The origin of entry into the Christian life begins with understanding our lost condition and damaged nature apart from God. Then a decision has to be made that acknowledges that lost condition, followed by voicing the content, substance ,and directed permission of that decision to commit to a relationship with Him. One way all of us give our permission is through the words we speak. Words give evidence to and reveal our beliefs and our will.

The voice of authority released with faith changes the fabric of your future because it simultaneously changes the condition of your spirit. With your words you authorize God to change your inner man, the being you truly are inside. The same way you give an auto technician permission to change out the engine in your car by your words, that's the same way you give God permission to change out the nature of your spirit. The difference is that you don't pay the bill for the change. It's already been paid for in Christ. All a person has to do is authorize it with the authority of their voice.

One fascinating thing about using your voice for giving permission is in the study of what's known as the unique "voiceprint" that a person possesses. To summarize, a person's voiceprint is the unique personal identifier carried within their voice—much like how a fingerprint is unique to a person. A voiceprint is the characteristic and quality of the human voice that is scientifically measurable and uniquely identifies each individual. The voiceprint characteristic is based on the physical makeup and the configuration of a person's mouth and throat. In other words, a person's voice is unique to them because of the shape of their vocal cavities, and because of the way they move their mouth when they speak. These characteristics are be expressed as a mathematical formula and be responsive to technological instruments. A computer software recognition program is projected to actually identify and authenticate a person on the basis of their voiceprint regardless of the words used for that recognition.

So from a scientific standpoint, our voice is a unique, personal identifier that authenticates our authority and our will in our lives. What we speak, what we confess with our mouths, is where we give our authorization to carry out our will revealed in our words. In connection with what we're looking at in Romans 10, our confession into salvation includes acknowledging Jesus died for our sins, but also that He was raised that we might walk in the light of His resurrection power, or as Paul describes in Romans 6, newness of life. We're not only saved from sin and all its consequences, but we're saved to eternal life and all its rewards, benefits, provisions and responsibilities.

> *Therefore we were buried with Him through baptism into death, that just as Christ was raised from the dead by the glory of the Father, even so we also should walk in newness of life. For if we have been united together in the likeness of His death, certainly we also shall be in the likeness of His resurrection. Knowing this, that our old man was crucified with Him, that the body of sin might be done away with, that we should no longer be slaves of sin. For he who has died has been freed from sin.*
>
> *Romans 6:4-7 NKJV*

When a person confesses Jesus as Lord, they're giving God permission to exchange their old condition and nature of sin for a new condition and nature of righteousness purchased by Christ and made anew in Christ. The words are the authorization for the immediacy of new life to be "installed" in a thorough replacement of the old man.

TRUTH #5: Because of the reality of eternal life, the re-born child of God is to aggressively, intentionally, and proactively use this divine law of confession to help them mature into the fullness of this new nature freely given by God. This includes, but is not limited to, the training of the spirit to speak with the voice of authority for material provisions, healing and health, a successful vocational

career and ministry, sound and fulfilling relationships, a good reputation with overall respectability, excellence and well-being in life.

At the moment of our new birth, the Spirit of God takes up full and permanent residence in the heart and life of the believer. Everything that was accomplished in Christ and through Christ is substantively lodged within the heart and life of the believer. Every spiritual blessing in heavenly places and all things that pertain to life and godliness are made available to the child of God. The fruit of the spirit are in place, access to the throne of grace and all that grace provides is given to us freely. We have the name, the authority and character of Jesus backing us in our daily lives.

With all that's been given to us, it's no wonder that Paul made it a point in Philemon 1:6 to tell us about one of the very important things that we must do about all these spiritual endowments given to us as believers.

That the sharing of your faith may become effective by the acknowledgement of every good thing which is in you in Christ Jesus.

Philemon 1:6 NKJV

There are two primary ways we share our faith. We share or express our faith in the words we speak and in the deeds we perform. In almost every case, words will precede deeds.

33

And our words must have corresponding actions that are in alignment with what we say or else we have faith that is dead, inactive, non-operative, and void of authority. To see the results of using the voice of authority accurately, we must act on what we say.

Thoughts and actions are certainly involved in the process of seeing change, but the focus of this point is on *the way we speak* about who we are in Christ, what we have in Christ and what we can do in Christ. We are given the responsibility to use the voice of authority in speaking to our circumstances that they conform to the truth of what it means to be in Christ. The common denominator in all we say must be "in Christ," or in the knowledge of what He has done and made available to us.

To be armed with knowledge of who we are in Christ is comparable to having a command from our Father in much the same way Jesus had a command from His Father about taking up His life for resurrection. We'll see more about these examples in coming chapters, but Jesus was not limited by circumstances that opposed the will of God in His life. He was confronted by obstacles and enemies, but He used the voice of authority to reject wrong thoughts, to calm winds and storms, to send away evil spirits, to rebuke sickness and demons, and to enforce healing and health. Circumstances didn't happen to Jesus so much as He happened to circumstances.

He took His faith in God and lived in line with this faith in God to speak from His heart what he believed in His heart. Jesus took fast and firm hold of scriptural and spiritual truth to make things around Him conform to that truth. He taught that the disciplined link between the heart and the mouth is the key to seeing change and "moving mountains."

For verily I say unto you, That whosoever shall say unto this mountain, Be thou removed and be thou cast into the sea; and shall not doubt in his heart, but shall believe that those things which he saith shall come to pass; he shall have whatsoever he saith.

Mark 11:23 KJV

Again, we'll go into greater detail on this spiritual law of confession described in Mark 11:23, but it is vitally important to note that, when it is repeatedly worked, this is a truth that will work repeatedly. The same way this truth has worked on small things, when we develop our use and masterery of this law, it will work on big things. This law of confession will work on natural things and spiritual things. There is no limitation found in this truth. The only limitation is how little or how much we live in exerting the authoritative voice of a speaking spirit based in sound, scriptural, spiritual authority. The limitation is contained within the level of belief and faith we develop in the heart— that is, how we develop in our belief and faith in God, and our belief and faith in His Word within the heart.

Paul asked the Galatians a very important question about their development in faith, particularly about why they limited themselves in faith.

This only I want to learn from you: Did you receive the Spirit by the works of the law, or by the hearing of faith? Are you so foolish? Having begun in the Spirit, are you now being made perfect by the flesh?

Galatians 3:2-3 NKJV

Paul was dealing with an issue that had arisen with the Galatians. They initially had accepted the work of Christ as superior to the law. They had an awareness of the provisions of grace over the law. But over time, there were those who re-introduced the law and proposed a mixture of law and grace. The problem was that the law was ineffective to produce righteousness or eternal life.

In Galatians 3:19, Paul wrote that one reason the law was added was for the purpose of revealing the sin nature and sin condition of man, so that when Jesus appeared, it would be evident that there was only one way out of sin and into eternal life. And that was in Christ. Galatians 3:24 goes on to say that the law was a schoolmaster or tutor, to bring the Jewish people and ultimately all the families of the earth into relationship with God through the gospel.

The point of his question in the first part of Galatians 3 was to awaken them to the fact that the way they began in Christ was the way they were to continue growing, developing and being perfected, or matured, in Christ.

When we as believers entered into relationship with God in Christ we used our voice backed by His authority to become children of God. It was also God's intention that we would engage the fullness of eternal life using the same law of confession to build and experience the life He's always intended for us. The voice of authority is how we got into Christ. The voice of authority is how we are to continue and excel in Christ.

How do we do this? To answer this question, we need to look into the next chapter to see and understand our example and standard as we define what is meant by the voice of authority. We'll also explain the value of one of the key tools Jesus used in teaching for understanding.

Chapter 2

What Is The Voice Of Authority?

So what do we mean by the "voice of authority?" Let's start by defining authority. In the New Testament, the English word "authority" is interpreted from the Greek word "exousia." This word means *"it is lawful, permission, liberty of doing as one pleases, the ability or strength with which one is endued, the right to exercise power and the power of one whose will and commands must be obeyed by others."*

Authority also means "the right to rule; the power to act, decide, command and judge." Having authority means you have the right to set policy, you have rights of rulership, you are in position to command subordinates, and you have the power to administer judgment to those who disobey commands or to reward those who conform to commands.

Authority is the right to use power and the rightful use of power. Biblical authority aims to influence others to produce a biblical, intended and godly result. Possessing authority is not the end goal. The use of power must be employed to do the right thing. The right use of authority is found in doing with it what must be done to demonstrate and enforce the will of God in the earth.

The word exousia also carries the meaning of "privilege to use ability, force, capacity, competency, freedom, mastery, delegated influence and jurisdiction." Speaking of the authority that a believer has, we could also define this as the "responsibility and expertise" of the believer. Considering all the facets and nuances of authority, it's an easy matter to see that we would greatly benefit from applying its meaning and values over the broad spectrum of our lives.

Applying the meaning of authority to the voice of a speaking spirit begins with understanding the intentions of God. With this in mind, the voice of authority is defined as "the verbally expressed will of God both in heaven and in earth that's released, commanded and established through the channel of decreed words."

The voice of authority is "the verbally expressed will of God both in heaven and in earth that's released, commanded and established through the channel of decreed words."

In many respects, the voice of authority is like the believer's right to issue a manifesto. A manifesto is "a public declaration of intentions, as by a government or political party or a written statement declaring publicly the intentions, motives, or views of the creator of policies, legislations or laws." So when God speaks His will, it's the manifested reality of His intentions, motives, and views being publicly declared.

In like manner, when a believer takes the will of God to speak, declare, and decree His will, it is done with the motive of manifesting and bringing into sight God's intentions. God backs His will and gives authority to His children to voice His will with confident expectation that it will come to pass.

So it's clear from scriptures that God has a will and He has authority to enforce and manifest or bring His will to pass. By the rights of creation and the bestowal of eternal life to people who have made the decision to accept salvation in Christ, God has children who are made in His image and likeness, given His nature and equipped with authority to manifest His will. As speaking spirits, God's children are equipped with a voice to decree His will with full authority and the full backing of heaven's corporate structure and power.

Anyone who follows the process outlined and presented here has a right to release the will of God with the voice of authority in the earth. This applies to things in life both small and great. This pertains to any circumstance of life, any issue that arises, any problem that demands a solution, or any question that seeks an answer. The voice of authority can be expressed to address relationships, health, finances, family, ministry, and career concerns.

In Mark 4, Jesus and His disciples encountered a trial that threatened their very lives. It followed a full day of work ministering to the multitudes. For hours Jesus had taught spiritual truth on how the kingdom of God operates, illustrating it with natural truth in the form of parables.

A parable is a story that takes a natural truth that people can clearly see from their everyday lives and explains that truth in such a way as to draw meaning from it in order to understand and apply spiritual truth in a practical way. In Mark 4, Jesus used seed, plants, crops, farming and a lamp to show how the kingdom of God functions and how to use this knowledge to live life in the earth like God always intended.

Mark 4:33-41 tells the story of what happened after the all-day teaching took place.

> *And with many such parables spake He the word unto them, as they were able to hear it. But without a parable spake He not unto them: and when they were alone, He expounded all things to His disciples. And the same day, when the even was come, He saith unto them, Let us pass over unto the other side. And when they had sent away the multitude, they took Him even as He was in the ship. And there were also with Him other little ships. And there arose a great storm of wind, and the waves beat into the ship, so that it was now full. And He was in the hinder part of the ship, asleep on a pillow: and they awake Him, and say unto Him, Master, carest thou not that we perish? And He arose, and rebuked the wind, and said unto the sea, Peace, be still. And the wind ceased, and there was a great calm. And He said unto them, Why are*

ye so fearful? How is it that ye have no faith? And they feared exceedingly, and said one to another, What manner of man is this, that even the wind and the sea obey Him?

Mark 4:33–41 KJV

In this passage we have one of the clearest demonstrations of the voice of authority in action. Let's keep in mind a few things Jesus said of Himself to keep proper perspective on what took place on this boat.

Jesus said of Himself, "I am the way, the truth and the life." So everything we see of Jesus is showing the right and best way to do things. There are many ways that seem right to a person, but the ends thereof lead to death, or separation from the right and best way. Any way that contradicts the ways Jesus modeled is ultimately separating a person from the way of living that will produce the best outcome.

When Jesus spoke and acted, it was all rooted in truth. In the place of the word truth, we could easily substitute the word "reality." So in essence, whatever Jesus said or did was the truest demonstration of the highest form and standard of reality. People say they just want to "keep it real," but anything of real meaning and true value begins and ends with the standard of reality that Jesus taught, lived, represented and expects of us.

The ultimate expression of life is found in Jesus. Life

has a quantity, a length and duration of days and measure of time. Life also has quality, a level of value, fulfillment, meaning, and reward. Life has a source that nourishes both the quantity and quality of a life. The source of life determines the quantity and quality of life. In the voice of authority, Jesus declared that He is the life source. But He also revealed His life source.

> *For as the Father has life in Himself, so He has granted the Son to have life in Himself, And has given Him authority to execute judgment also, because He is the Son of Man.*
>
> *John 5:26-27 NKJV*

Even though He was perfectly God and man, Jesus acknowledged that His life flowed from God the Father, the source of all life. Jesus also knew and understood His place of authority, and that He had been granted authority over life as a whole and over His own life personally. He was also given authority to execute, or enforce, judgment over eternal life. Jesus was making it known that He would be the entry point and evaluator for a person to receive and experience eternal life.

Hebrews 5:9 backs this up saying, *"And having been perfected, He (Jesus) became the author of eternal salvation to all who obey Him."* The word "author" is a root for the word "authority." So we could just as easily say that Jesus became not only the originator, but the authority of eternal salvation for all who obey Him.

One more thought to include for perspective on what was taking place in the boat in Mark 4 is another statement Jesus said of Himself: *"If you've seen Me, you've seen the Father."* Jesus was saying that He was and is the perfect revelation of the will of God for all people and for all time. Jesus was and is the perfect expression of the theology, meanings and purposes of God. He was and is the perfect embodiment and demonstration of the intentions, motives and views of God.

With this perspective in mind, let's look at Mark 4:33-41 in more detail. If we can see what Jesus did, we can learn the scriptural way, standard of reality, and source of life necessary to do work in the earth how Jesus did work. If we can get the image and pattern of how and why Jesus released the voice of authority and revealed the will of God in that boat, we likewise can see how to influence real time events in the earth. And we can do the same types of things in our own lives.

And with many such parables He spoke the word to them as they were able to hear it.

Mark 4:33 NKJV

Other translations of this verse say, "so far as they were able to receive it," and "according to their capacity for receiving it," and "such as their minds could take in." Jesus used parables to help expand the capacity of the hearer to get more understanding about what He was teaching. He frequently gave His message in parables with a purpose to communicate a specific objective. Jesus always spoke with a defined direction in mind and with authenticity and selflessness from His heart. Where did this direction come from and how did it come?

> *Then Jesus answered and said to them, "Most assuredly, I say to you, the Son can do nothing of Himself, but what He sees the Father do; for whatever He does, the Son also does in like manner.*
>
> *John 5:19 NKJV*

Every parent knows the power of influence on children. Children will imitate things they see on television or in others and most greatly what they see in their parents. Jesus said He did nothing without first seeing it in the Father. A child feels most authorized to act when he or she is acting like their parents. This is what makes parenting one of the greatest responsibilities that exists. A parent—or an authority figure—models the way of life and truth in life to a child and sets an image of how to develop, mature and reproduce in the generations to follow.

Jesus saw the standard of reality demonstrated by His Father and He modeled that standard for every generation of humanity to follow. He made it intimately clear that His agenda was not His own but His manner of life originated with His Father's will and purposes. Jesus made it very clear that He didn't come with any hidden agendas. His will was a mirror image of His Father's will. His message was a transparent communication of the Father's heart and will.

> *I can of Myself do nothing. As I hear, I judge; and My judgment is righteous, because I do not seek My own will but the will of the Father who sent Me.*
>
> *John 5:30 NKJV*

> *Jesus answered them and said, "My doctrine is not Mine, but His Who sent Me."*
>
> *John 7:16 NKJV*

Operating in this understanding is what energized Jesus' authority. This behavior dynamically empowered His voice. Jesus made it His business to be sensitive to the plans that God wanted carried out in the earth. He prioritized His awareness of what God was saying to Him. He developed His message from the conversations He had with God. He focused His speech to speak from the body and content of what God delivered to Him and taught Him.

> *I have many things to say and to judge concerning you, but He who sent Me is true; and I speak to the world those things which I heard from Him."*

They did not understand that He spoke to them of the Father. Then Jesus said to them, "When you lift up the Son of Man, then you will know that I am He, and that I do nothing of Myself; but as My Father taught Me, I speak these things.

John 8:26-28 NKJV

This was Jesus' way of life for a lifetime. He always spoke with a purpose. He refused to waste His time or His words. We can look at his life from the gospels and come to the conclusion that He enjoyed life. He ate and drank. He went to dinner parties and fellowshipped with people. He built relationships.

At the same time He made it known that the message He was given by the Father was to be well communicated and accurately spoken to the world through His words and His life. This message was revealing the heart and will of God as a Father, God as Lover of the people He created. He wanted this message of love spread throughout the world and Jesus knew He was the messenger, message, and example of that love.

Jesus knew He was the pattern, Son and the demonstration of eternal life. Jesus was taught what to say by the Father's example to Him, and He followed the instructions and example of that message wholeheartedly. This approach to life is what put substance in His voice and effectiveness in the authority released through His voice.

> *For I have not spoken of My own authority; but the*
> *Father Who sent Me gave Me a command, what I*
> *should say, and what I should speak. And I know that*
> *His command is everlasting life. Therefore, whatever*
> *I speak, just as the Father has told Me, so I speak.*

> *John 12:49-50 NKJV*

Jesus explained that His message and how he was to communicate this message was a personal commandment from God telling Him the methods to use in speaking. You remember Jesus said, "If you've seen me, you've seen the Father?" In John 12:49-50, Jesus was essentially saying, "If you've heard me, you've heard the Father."

Jesus understood that when He spoke and ministered He represented the heart and will of God, and also the image and picture people would get of God. This is one reason He taught in parables, or word picture stories.

> *But without a parable He did not speak to them. And*
> *when they were alone, He explained all things to His*
> *disciples.*

> *Mark 4:34 NKJV*

The first part of Mark 4:34 says, *"But without a parable He did not speak to them..."* One translation of this says *"He said nothing to them except in* figures.*"* The capacity, or ability to hear, connects with figures or pictures. Jesus was painting pictures and developing images so people could see things beyond where they were. In learning, we always start with what we know to help make the connections with things we don't know. In the process of this, we don't see with our eyes alone, we see with our minds and the experiences and perspectives of our lives.

One thing that's true for sure is that a person can't move beyond the actual image they have within themselves. A person can only go as far as they can see themselves going. In life, we don't see things as they are. We see things as we are.

Remember the 12 spies in Numbers 13-14? They were sent to survey the land that God promised to Abraham and his descendants. Moses was in leadership after Israel had spent centuries as slaves in Egypt. Now they had been set free from their captivity and were poised to enter a new era of promise and prosperity.

All 12 of these spies saw the prosperity of the land promised to them, but 10 came back with doubts that they could defeat the people and take the land as their own. In fact, they inflated the people of the land to be giants and reduced themselves to the size of grasshoppers in the sight of the inhabitants of the land. That wasn't the case in reality. But the point is that's how the spies saw themselves and their newly formed nation compared to the people of the land they were to conquer.

They didn't see things for the way they truly were or else the 10 would have agreed with Joshua and Caleb, the other two sent on this mission with them. Joshua and Caleb saw things the way God saw things, the way it had been spoken to them. Because they held fast to God's promise and God's will, Joshua and Caleb saw themselves properly and they saw their circumstances accurately.

As a nation at that time, Israel collectively couldn't go beyond what they could see. What's the lesson to be learned? If you can't see things differently than you currently see them, you can't go where you would like to go, or perhaps even are destined to go. Because of the limited ability to see how God saw things, these ten leaders limited what was available and possible for an entire nation. And unfortunately, it took decades to change the image of what Israel saw, and subsequently experienced, as a nation.

New things—new ideas and new opportunities—come to people's lives all the time. Some see things for what they are and what they can be to them, and some don't. When Christopher Columbus and others of his century presented the belief that the world was round, many scoffed at the notion. There were those of that time who genuinely believed the earth was flat and if you sailed far enough across the sea you would get to the edge of the earth and drop off into a great and unending chasm. Until it was proven false, this belief limited travel and exploration.

Far too many people are "flat world" motivated. They see the limitations in life and style their way of living to accommodate the limitations. When you see the world as round you lift untrue limitations and you can travel much further than you ever dreamed was possible. I'm not talking about unrealistic pursuits. I'm talking about the barriers people construct within, or the voices from outside that tell us we can never go beyond the life we currently live.

A barracuda is bred by nature to kill its prey for food. If you put a clear, see-through barrier in a fish tank between a barracuda and its food, the barracuda will try to break through the invisible barrier to eat, but after a certain number of times of hitting the barrier between itself and its opportunities for provision, the barracuda will stop trying to go beyond the barrier. You can even remove the "see through" partition, and the barracuda won't try to cross that invisible barrier because of its previous conditioning.

If we don't press through to acquire new and better knowledge, our past experiences, pre-shaped perspectives and pre-conditioned beliefs in life can restrict us to stay separated from our answers, rights, and blessings, despite them being within our reach.

How we see things will determine how far we're able to go in life and what barriers we'll break through. Our perspectives and beliefs affect our capacity to see, hear, learn, receive and grow. People reject new information for any number of reasons. Some limit themselves because they don't like the channel through which new knowledge is being broadcast. Sometimes it's because of the way a thing is being presented. Some like things that are more entertaining. Some like things that are more scholarly. When you boil it all down, none of those things should matter as much as getting what's needed.

To reject new knowledge on the basis of not liking or relating to the person delivering it would be comparable to a man dying of thirst but refusing water that could save his life because the cup is the wrong size, wrong shape or wrong color in his thinking and to his liking. If you were thirsting to death for water and came across a water well with a certain color vessel, you would be foolish to reject the life-giving, refreshing waters of the well because of the size, shape or color of the vessel being lowered into the well to gather those waters.

Some people reject the word of God on the basis of their like or dislike of the vessel presenting the Word. Or they refuse it on the basis of the way it's delivered to them. Consequently, their beliefs and level of maturity stay the same.

Jesus knows that most people are hard pressed to change their beliefs and mature if they don't have a picture to cling to in building a new image within. This is one reason why He used parables so readily. Speaking of this same story in

Mark 4, Matthew writes:

> *All these things spake Jesus unto the multitudes in parables; and without a parable spake He not unto them: That it might be fulfilled which was spoken by the prophet, saying, "I will open My mouth in parables; I will utter things which have been kept secret from the foundation of the world."*
>
> *Matthew 13:34-35 KJV*

This reference in Matthew 13:35 was a quote of Psalm 78:2, which one translation interprets, "I will utter things concealed since Creation." Jesus' use of parables was done in following the Father's will. *He used the teaching path of parables to reveal ancient truths held back until that day and age.* There were truths about God, about eternal life, about His kingdom and His ways that couldn't be fully appreciated until the need for those things was understood. In using parables, Jesus was communicating things established from ancient times, from the earliest times as created by God "in the beginning."

The greatest illustration of this is the plan of redemption. It's hard to help someone who lacks the awareness that they even need help in some area of their life. Man needed help, but man was determined to help himself apart from God. Man didn't have a comprehension of eternal life and the consequences of being disconnected from the nature of

God through sin.

God gave the law as a means to understand the measuring stick required to be met in order to have eternal life. No one measured up to the stick until Jesus. The law and Jesus were presented in contrast to one another to help man understand his need for a Savior, and to see that Jesus met the requirements of the law and was the answer to the problem. God had to define the problem and the need so that the solution would be understood by man.

Matthew 13 is a chapter filled with parables Jesus taught. In particular, the parables of tares, of hidden treasure, of the pearl of great price and of the net, are all describing how the kingdom of God operates in relation to redemption made available to man.

In the parable of tares, people have a choice to be a harvest of fruitful grain—of wheat—and thereby, be part of the salvation purchased in Christ. In the parable of hidden treasure, people have the choice to be among those who search out the most precious things given to us in redemption, and to also make sacrifices to bring other "precious fruit" into the kingdom. In the parable of the pearl of great price, people have a choice to recognize the immense value of one soul brought into the kingdom and be immersed in the pursuit of winning souls.

In the parable of the net, everyone will one day be a part of either the good or bad creatures caught from the sea of humanity, and every individual will personally determine if they will be numbered with the just and be free of eternal punishment or if they will be with the unjust who will be sent to the furnace of fire that burns forever.

Every parable has a purpose, and within every purpose, there is an answer to an urgent need. In a practical, every day way, we would benefit from thinking that when a need arises, the solution is present. Many times people can panic when a problem appears, but to the one who looks to God, there's an answer within reach. You've probably heard it said that "necessity is the mother of invention." That's certainly been proven time and time again. When need is kept in proper perspective, it motivates ingenuity, creativity, vision, and awareness. And frequently, things that are already in the environment are the solution to a current problem or need.

Sometimes the value of things aren't recognized or properly utilized until the time of need arises. How long has electricity existed in the atmosphere? How long has oil been in the earth? How long have the raw materials for computer chips been around? When were the mathematical and scientific laws and principles we use today first available to humanity? When were these things discovered?

One aspect of the answer to these questions is that these things were discovered when man's knowledge matured to the point of understanding the foundations necessary to comprehend the new knowledge we have today. Another aspect of the answer is that these things were discovered when the time of need arose to take full advantage of the knowledge.

God is again releasing ancient truths held back until this day and age in which we live. The voice of authority is revelation of truth that has been made known anew in our day.

Jesus used parables in this way. Parables helped to mature awareness of the old knowledge and to help people learn about and develop in the use of new knowledge. Parables also helped allow for the uncovering of things whose time of need had arisen in the earth. The time came where machines and cars required refined oil and gasoline to fuel easier and faster ways of travel and a great number of other activities for civilized progress.

In like fashion, these parables Jesus taught helped to ignite awareness, understanding, and experience of the kingdom of God in Jesus' day. These parables, and others that relate to modern progress, can help do the same in our day.

At the core of this way of teaching, Jesus' parable driven messages built images in the hearts and minds of the listeners. They were designed to activate a law of dominant images, expand the boundaries, and lift the limitations in the lives of the hearers. This law of dominant images says that, "You and the events of your life will always go in the direction of the most dominant thoughts and images you allow to reside in your heart and mind."

The twelve spies spoken of earlier demonstrated this law. The ten had contradictory thoughts and images that were greater in their hearts and minds than what God had stated as His will. God had promised the land to Israel by covenant. He told Moses the land was theirs to take. But the ten, who were national leaders, had images within that opposed both what their eyes saw for the taking and what their ears had heard about God's promise. These ten leaders fed the image of a nation and millions were limited and restricted from experiencing the very thing God had promised and authorized them to have.

Joshua and Caleb were different. They both had thoughts and images that were rooted in God's will. This gave authority to do exploits mighty enough to take the land. They both decreed that the people that would oppose them were like bread for them to eat and that their enemy's defenses were incapable of stopping Israel from taking what was rightfully promised them as part of God's covenant with Abraham and God's will for Abraham's descendants.

God taught Abraham the power of having vision to see beyond where he was. God trained Abraham to build an image within of what He said. Abraham wasn't flawlessly perfect along the way. There were times where he made more of what he could see naturally than what he could see with the eyes of his heart, but Abraham did come to have what God promised through keeping right images alive inside. The training began when he and his nephew, Lot, had a problem over land and space for their herds to graze and grow. Abram, as he was known at this point, chose the high road to refuse strife from developing between himself and Lot and gave Lot the best of the land that was available.

> *After Lot left, God began speaking to Abram. And the Lord said to Abram, after Lot had separated from him: "Lift your eyes now and look from the place where you are—northward, southward, eastward, and westward; For all the land which you see I give to you and your descendants forever. And I will make your descendants as the dust (sand) of the earth; so that if a man could number the dust (sand) of the earth, then your descendants also could be numbered.*
>
> *Genesis 13:14-16 NKJV*

Look carefully at what God said to Abram. He said, "Lift up your eyes, because everything you can see from where you are today is yours to have and use." God was saying to Abram that the land was within the scope of his God-given authority to have, possess, and experience. God specifically said that all the land was going to be given to Abram and his seed, descendants.

What he could experience wasn't limited to what he might have taken in with his physical eyes, but ultimately included every place the sole of his foot would tread, every place that God directed him, and every place that his heart and mind could comprehend.

God was putting before Abram's eyes the sights necessary to create the reality of his future. We must do the same thing. This has to be done physically, and just as significantly, it has to be done with the images that we see within. That's where the parables come into play.

Notice in Genesis 13:16, God said, "And I will make thy seed as the dust of the earth..." This was a parable like use of an image with which Abram could easily relate. In that part of the world, the dust or sand, was plentiful. Abram would have seen grains of sand just about every day of his life. So every time he saw sand, he would have a visual reminder of the promise of God. Every time he saw sand, the image was reinforced and grew stronger.

That's what a parable is designed to do. Parables present visual reminders within the heart and mind of the promise and operations of God, causing images to grow more dominant within us each time we hear the parable or see a representation of the natural truth used in a parable.

If you're still not convinced that this thought about parables and images is significant, you need only investigate the negative side of the process for a moment. Serial murderers have testified that they began their downward spiral into a violent reality with an unhindered addiction to pornography. Through wrong images, the human body was devalued and the heart of the viewer was desensitized to the personality, rights, value, needs and desires of others. Over time the conscience became seared and violent. Degrading images were held within with greater and greater strength until the direction of the images were acted out. If it works with such intensity negatively, it will work with the same degree and even more greatly in a positive, productive and godly way.

Through understanding parables—representative and powerful pictures of a specific truth—we can understand how the kingdom of God operates and grow in comprehending God's will. The more we cultivate insight to His will for our lives personally, the more effective we can be in releasing the voice of authority in our lives. As we look further into the voice of authority in action, pay particular attention to not only what Jesus said but why He was confident in speaking with authority.

We have two primary objectives for the next chapters:

1. Illustrate how Jesus used the voice of authority in the earth.

2. Show how you can use it to transform the quality of your life here in the earth.

I highlight these key objectives so that the goal is very clear. By enhancing your powers of concentration and focus on this goal, I believe you will achieve greater value from these next chapters. I also believe focused application of what's contained here will prove beneficial in the short term and long term experiences of your life.

Chapter 3

How This Voice Is Shaped

S o we see that the voice of authority is defined as the verbally expressed will of God both in heaven and in earth, which is released, commanded, and established through the channel of decreed words. In the following chapters, we'll help to put even more foundation in place to understand and operate in the voice of authority most effectively. What we want to look at now is what the voice of authority looks and sounds like in action and what shapes it to be so powerful.

In Mark 4, after teaching all day, Jesus spent time alone with His disciples. The latter part of Mark 4:34 says "… and when they were alone, he expounded all things to his disciples." Other translations say, he explained things "privately to his disciples." The Amplified Bible says, "…and when they were in private, He explained everything fully."

It was in private sessions like these that Jesus would explain further the things He had been teaching. I imagine that He would answer questions and add more illustrations, or remind the disciples of things He had said. I believe it was in these times together that Jesus would seek to fill in the gaps between what they understood about what He was teaching and where He needed them to be in their understanding.

Jesus wasn't telling the most private things to the multitudes but to those who were committed and close to Him. In the same way, God doesn't tell His greatest secrets to those who are distant from Him. You have to be close to hear a whisper, and there are times when God whispers His secrets in the ears of those who are close enough to hear Him.

God doesn't share His most intimate secrets with the casual Christian. God's not speaking the confidential information about His operations to the one who disrespects or mocks Him. He's not divulging strategic knowledge to the one who visits the secret place on rare and inconsistent occasions. This isn't to say that God's hiding His insights from people, but I am emphasizing that the condition of hearing is met through proximity to God and the priority God holds in people's lives. When it's truly important, a person will come close enough to hear what's being said or search diligently enough to find the knowledge they need.

When God speaks, He does it with a purpose in mind. He speaks for people to believe what He says and take action on what He says. After Jesus had taught all day and followed it up with a private time of mentorship and instructing with the disciples, Jesus had an important instruction of His own to follow what had come from the Father. They had to cross the sea and arrive in the country of the Gadarenes.

On the same day, when evening had come, He said to them, "Let us cross over to the other side."

Mark 4:35 NKJV

It's important to remember that this is the evening of the same day, when He gave His message in parables to build the whole image on several important topics through the Word of God. Jesus taught that day on how the kingdom of God operated in the earth, how to be productive and victorious in life, how to apply the Word of God to mature and become greater than the circumstances of life, how to become a help for others in their time of need, and how to produce specifically desired results through the Word of God.

After fully explaining the inside understanding and insights of these truths to His disciples, on the same day as all of this teaching, Jesus said, "Let us pass over to the other side." Jesus had taught the multitudes that "The sower sows the word." Luke 8:11 says, "Now the parable is this: The seed is the word of God." Jesus had taught them that words function like seeds. Words produce what's in them. Words mature and ripen based upon the content and substance contained within them. Words materialize in sight what they're designed to become. Over time, words develop into a visible state that becomes tangible and experienced.

Jesus was making the point that based on the Word of God, you have to speak what you want to come to pass. You can't speak in a natural sense what you see that's undesired, and you can't speak your doubts and expect things to change.

In speaking the words, "Let us pass over to the other side," Jesus decreed an outcome. It was aligned in the same fashion and authority like when God said, "Let there be light." It was His desired will and expected result. Jesus stated what was possible to anyone who believed it. Even if the boat sank and He had to walk the rest of the way, Jesus was going to cross over to the other side.

Think about it. This word, "*Let* us cross over to the other side," was personally spoken to them. They had every right to claim it, stand on it, speak it, remind God about it, and act and talk in a way that corresponded with this word that had been sown into their lives and into their futures. Jesus was speaking truthfully what He wanted. He was casting vision of a future reality to come to pass. He was guiding the disciples by giving them His instructions. He was showing them things to come in a personal and intimate way. This is what God does for believers today through the voice of His Spirit.

Howbeit when He, the Spirit of truth, is come, He will guide you into all truth: for He shall not speak of Himself; but whatsoever He shall hear, that shall He speak: and He will show you things to come.

John 16:13 KJV

When Jesus was on the earth, He spoke to the world what the Father wanted said and He spoke personally to those close to Him. Today, He frequently speaks to us through the Holy Spirit. The New King James version states John 16:13 this way: "However, when He, the Spirit of truth, has come, He will guide you into all truth; for He will not speak on His own authority, but whatever He hears He will speak; and He will tell you things to come."

In order to hear what He's saying about things to come, we have to draw close and have an ear to hear. Jesus specifically said, "He who has ears to hear, let him hear!" To Jesus, there was a sense of urgency that we be positioned to where hearing could take place.

While teaching these parables, Jesus also made another key statement in Mark 4:24-26 that renders a clue to operating in the voice of authority. "Take heed what you hear. With the same measure you use, it will be measured to you, and to you who hear, more will be given. For whoever has, to him more will be given; but whoever does not have, even what he has will be taken away from him."

In regards to these statements about having ears to hear and taking heed of what you hear, it wasn't and isn't just a matter of having physical ears. It's a matter of being in the places where you can hear the right things and positioning yourself to give the proper measure of respect and action to what you hear. In Luke's account of this story, Jesus said,

"Take heed how you hear." The mocking, disinterested, skeptical hearer will have one level of understanding, but the reverent, focused, believing hearer is going to get a level of understanding that excels. The latter group has a promise of getting more understanding and insight, plus productive directions, while the former group will lose the little bit they may have heard if changes aren't made in respect to what they hear.

Consider how Jesus did things in relation to His hearing. Isaiah 50:4 says, "The Lord God has given Me the tongue of the learned, that I should know how to speak a word in season to him who is weary. He awakens Me morning by morning, He awakens My ear to hear as the learned." Jesus would have read about how God had given him the ear of the learned and the tongue of a learned disciple to speak with a voice in the earth that carried authority over distress. He would have known that day by day, morning by morning He had to open His ear to hear as the learned. And what He learned is what He said.

In Psalm 40:6-9, Jesus would have read, "...My ears you have opened. Then said I, Behold, I come: In the volume of the book it is written of Me. I delight to do Your will, O My God, and your law is within My heart...Indeed, I do not restrain My lips." Jesus found His life's purpose and directions for His day to day life through the Book—the scrolls that contained the scriptures. He looked to God to open His ears to hear and learn directly from the volume of the Book how to live and operate in the earth.

Imagine picking up the scrolls that contained the scriptures from God and seeing for the first time God's words about you. This is what Jesus went through. By reading the written scriptures, He repeatedly gained ground in learning about Himself, about His calling, function and destiny. He also gained understanding that God would continually speak to Him through these scriptures, and that God would daily speak to Him directly through the voice of His Spirit.

Look at what Jesus read of the ultimate sacrifice He would make in fulfilling the plan of redemption. Jesus took heed to what He heard, but also how he heard it. This is how He prepared Himself for the most difficult times of His life.

The Lord God has opened My ear; and I was not rebellious, nor did I turn away. I gave My back to those who struck Me, and My cheeks to those who plucked out the beard; I did not hide My face from shame and spitting. For the Lord God will help Me; therefore I will not be disgraced; therefore I have set My face like a flint, and I know that I will not be ashamed.

Isaiah 50:5-7 NKJV

Many times, people try to speak with the voice of authority but have done little to prepare within for the battles that will come from outside. Jesus had a game plan in place so that when the time came to live this out, He was ready, equipped, and strengthened. Jesus operated His authority from the basis of both the written word and the word spoken in His heart. Jesus exercised the voice of authority on the basis of the two—working together as one. He made decisions on how to live *before* the time of testing, not just during the time of testing or following a time of testing. This is how He heard the word with the ear of the learned. This is how He spoke with the tongue of the learned in a voice filled with authority.

If we take the time to have ears to hear, God will likewise open our ears to have the ear of the learned. What we hear will give instruction to our tongue. Our tongue becomes that of the learned. The plain truth is this: Just like with Jesus, it is written of us in the volume of the book. We can and should operate our authority on the basis of what's written in the scriptures and by what's spoken in our hearts. Doing things this way gives spiritual credibility and heaven backed power to speak with the voice of authority.

John 16:13-15 shows how the chain of communication and command works to produce the voice of authority. God speaks to Jesus. Jesus speaks to the Holy Spirit. The Holy Spirit speaks to us.

However, when He, the Spirit of truth, has come, He will guide you into all truth; for He will not Speak on His own authority, but whatever He hears He will speak; and He will tell you things to come. He will glorify Me, for He will take of what is Mine and declare it to you. All things that the Father has are Mine. Therefore I said that He will take of Mine and declare it to you.

John 16:13-15 NKJV

Armed with knowledge from the Spirit of Truth guiding us into all truth and showing us things to come, we speak to our current and future circumstances backed by the authority of the Father, Son, and Holy Spirit. Our voice of authority is released in cooperation with scriptural principles and spiritual laws. The voice of authority we speak with activates spiritual machinery and engages the help of angelic assistance. Our words prompt and energize our actions, shape our conduct, and bolster our behaviors to be consistent with what we say in the voice of authority.

Think it through: the Father speaks to Jesus who in turn speaks to the Holy Spirit, who then speaks to each of us what is to be personally said to us, about us. This is when and where personal information is communicated to us from God about our ordained, or authorized, place in the world. It's where He reveals our purpose and destiny. As we draw closer to hear His voice, we come to understand our personal themes, campaigns and causes in life.

In the context of this, there are times where a direct word seems to flow to our heart from God as our Father, or Jesus as our Lord and Savior, or the Holy Spirit as our

Teacher and Comforter. There are times where what God is speaking to us is communicated through different aspects of the Godhead yet never loses the integrity of this chain of communication.

As God speaks to us in this fashion, this is also where personal commandments are given to apply to our personal, everyday routines and circumstances. The personal commands are the things God says that are meaningful to us but may not trigger the same response in others. God may tell us certain ways to eat, things to stop or start, projects to put on hold, or people to connect with or withdraw from. These things may not motivate others to join your walk in the same direction, but for you, it's just as important as the written Word on a matter. You might present it for the consideration of others, but you don't make your personal command a law to others. You apply it to your life for your benefit and well-being and enjoy the fruit of it.

For example, there was a season of time in my life some years ago where I was feeling run down, exhausted, and continually fatigued. I sought to take a little extra time off, to get extra sleep, but none of that seemed to be helping much at all.

But one day, I heard a word in my spirit, "Drink your way out of this." This is the kind of statement I'd better explain further. Without really recognizing it, I had become dehydrated. But in hearing that phrase, "Drink your way out of this," I had the distinct impression that I needed to amend and improve the types of fluids I was drinking on a daily basis. I began drinking more good and purified water. I incorporated green tea, electrolyte drinks, and some probiotic drinks into my regimen. I didn't do this as a one-time thing for a few hours one day, I continued replenishing my body over a sustained period of time with good fluids, and I felt much better rather quickly.

This was a personal command I received and respected as coming from the Lord spoken to my heart. It wasn't necessarily something I needed to mandate in others' lives. Certainly, it's a good thing to be aware of putting the right and best kinds of fluids into your body as a general principle, but the steps I needed to take weren't for everyone. But this was a life-changing event for me.

There was another time several years ago, I was going through a difficult time physically with an intense back pain. The pain was so constant and prominent that it made it very difficult to sleep. One morning, drifting out of a couple hours of sleep into the morning time, I heard these words, "If he rests, he will recover." Then I heard another voice, "Will he do it?" The reply was, "Yes, he will."

But that wasn't the end of the story. While seeking the Lord further, I was impressed to read the book of Mark in its entirety every day. Then I got added instruction to verbally record the book of Mark in my own voice and continue to read Mark daily while listening to my voice reading it. This went on for a short season of time and was accompanied by another instruction to incorporate a specific nutritional supplement. The Word and the supplements alleviated the pain, which in turn gave me strength and relief to sleep and rest, and in a matter of a few days I recovered from something that had bothered me for an extended period of time.

Whether it's great, sweeping, life-changing directions He gives us, or personal directions to follow that remove the small foxes before they can grow up, it's with the ear of the learned that we are to hear His will and His Word. Whether written in the scriptures or spoken in our hearts in line with the scriptures, God's will is God's Word and this is our place of authority. It's with the ear of the learned that we are to speak with the tongue of the learned and in the voice of authority. And doing these things with a sense of regularity will grow and build the voice of authority in you.

Chapter 4

Journey Across the Sea

And the same day, when the even was come, He saith unto them, Let us pass over unto the other side. And when they had sent away the multitude, they took Him even as He was in the ship. And there were also with Him other little ships.

Mark 4:35-36 KJV

After teaching all day, the multitudes were sent away, and Jesus gave directions to cross over to the other side. The Word was sown throughout the day to the multitudes, then privately with the disciples. It was being sown again as the disciples boarded the ship. Faith had come as a ready passenger to travel with the disciples. Jesus was on the ship, too, but obviously tired from a full day of ministry. Not only was the boat that carried the disciples traveling to the other side of the sea, but other little ships were traveling with them.

This brings up another generally important point about operating in the voice of authority. There are others depending on you to take your place, fulfill your role, and exercise authority in your sphere of influence. Be it in your family, area of work, or ministry, those under your jurisdiction are looking to you to contribute to their safety and well-being. This isn't to excuse other people's responsibilities and the exercise of their own authority, but leaders of every capacity and every role must do their part to develop the voice of authority.

Staying under the sphere of influence to which you're assigned, and being found in your rightful place are keys to your authority being effectively deployed. This means respecting and submitting to the authority under which God places you. It also means respecting their words and directions, even in stressful and challenging times.

And there arose a great storm of wind, and the waves beat into the ship, so that it was now full.

Mark 4:37 KJV

As the disciples were navigating across the sea in cooperation with what Jesus said, they met resistance. A storm arose. This word for "arose" means "to cause to be, to be generated and come into being." There was some unseen and sudden force at work creating this storm, because the implication was that this storm appeared out of nowhere, without the type of foreseeable warning that would accompany a tempest of such proportions. You ever heard the phrase, "that just came out of the nowhere" *or* "out of the blue"? It means that things were clear and then, "wham!" It was like being blindsided and knocked for a loop. That's how this storm developed—suddenly, quickly, and with great ferocity and force.

One thing that makes this so unusual is that some of the disciples were seasoned fishermen who would have understood the seas and weather signs. They would have had some sense of a storm on the horizon. If there were indications of a storm and no one else had said anything, I think Peter would have spoken up when Jesus said, "*Let's go to the other side of the sea.*"

So out of nowhere came the "perfect storm." Mark 4:37 describes it as a "*great*" storm. The word for great is *megas* and means "exceedingly great, greatest, high, large, loud and mighty." This storm sounded like a great tornado, like a freight train rumbling through a tunnel.

Let's consider the full meaning of some of the other words in this verse. The word for storm means "whirlwind, squall and tempest." The word for wind means "wind by implication from the four quarters of the earth; to blow air." The Amplified Bible says, "A furious storm of wind (of hurricane proportions) arose. From these descriptive meanings, we can see that this was no ordinary storm.

This storm arose specifically to challenge, oppose and overturn the words Jesus voiced, "Let us pass over to the other side," and in a general sense, to uproot the words

Jesus had been teaching throughout the day. Remember the parable of the sower? What are the enemy's specific tactics to extract power and effectiveness from the Word of God?

And these are the ones by the wayside where the word is sown. When they hear, Satan comes immediately and takes away the word that was sown in their hearts. These likewise are the ones sown on stony ground who, when they hear the word, immediately receive it with gladness; And they have no root in themselves, and so endure only for a time. Afterward, when tribulation or persecution arises for the word's sake, immediately they stumble. Now these are the ones sown among thorns; they are the ones who hear the word, And the cares of this world, the deceitfulness of riches, and the desires for other things entering in choke the word, and it becomes unfruitful. But these are the ones sown on good ground, those who hear the word, accept it, and bear fruit: some thirtyfold, some sixty, and some a hundred.

Mark 4:15-20 NKJV

Notice that with the wayside type of ground, Satan came immediately to steal the word that was sown. Speaking of the same parable, Matthew 13:19 puts it this way. *"When anyone hears the word of the kingdom and does not understand it, then the wicked one comes and snatches away what was sown in his heart."* From what happened on the boat, the enemy used several of the tactics Jesus explained. Because the disciples had a limited range of fully understanding everything that Jesus had been teaching that day, he began using affliction and care with a good strong dose of fear, panic, confusion and chaos to distract and snatch away everything Jesus had taught that day and later imparted to the disciples when they were together privately.

It's interesting to note that facing adversity potentially has a way of imposing a short-term amnesia to our mind and faith if we allow it. Sometimes, we forget we have access to the very tools and authority to resist and overcome adversity. That's an aspect of how a lack of understanding is demonstrated. Understanding that's strongly ingrained becomes a part of an automatic response system when adversity and crisis arises. It's much like the reflex response we have when a doctor taps just below the knee cap with that little rubber hammer. The pressure point in the knee responds with a jerk forward when it faces outside pressure. This is what ingrained understanding can do when we face hardship, bad reports, tough times, or a crisis of any sort. Instead of shrinking back, we responsively jerk forward to attack a crisis with faith, authority, and biblically proven solutions.

Given this automatic response to crisis, it doesn't eliminate the pain and confusion a crisis may bring. Crisis brings pressure, and the disciples were in a crisis and under pressure, for sure. Pressure through people is categorized as persecution, while pressure from circumstances is affliction.

The disciples were being afflicted, and this was choking out any opportunity for the Word that was sown in their hearts to dominate their circumstances. If we find ourselves in a crisis, it's important to remember that faith doesn't put pressure on people to solve their problems. Faith speaks in the voice of authority, believes God and His word, and exerts pressure against circumstances.

Years ago, I was with a team of people flying into Dallas-Fort Worth from the West Coast. All of a sudden, we were afflicted with major and unusual turbulence and experienced a significant altitude drop over what seemed a prolonged period, great enough that it caused several of us to come close to hitting our heads on the overhead luggage bin. I was alarmed but had a sense of peace, remembering that before boarding the plane, I had said, "Let us pass over safely to our destination." We arrived safely, and these words, along with the faith of others, played a part in that sense of peace.

There are times in life where you may feel the storms are greatly against you, like the winds of adversity have gathered together against you from the four corners of the earth. It's like circumstances are creating a whirlwind effect, and your life is swirling out of control, but remember the words, "Let us pass over to the other side," and remember the impact and authority of "Peace, be still."

When you speak with the voice of authority to express what God puts in your heart, there will be opposition or resistant forces to some degree, and at times, it may be great, but remember, "Greater is He that is in you than he that is in the world." You may have financial difficulties or even financial disasters, but surround yourself with words and evidence from the scriptures that your God will supply all your need. In those moments, continue to say, "The Lord will provide!" There may be times where you've been treated unfairly and unjustly. Recall to mind what the Lord says, and declare it out loud: "Vengeance is mine. I will repay." Just make sure you're not helping the opposition with poorly researched or even bad decisions. Make sure you're not contributing and consenting to the difficulties being faced.

When storms come—and it's not being in doubt to be aware that storms will come—just remember these are tactics of resistance and diversion from the enemy or environment, but you don't have to participate in the tactics. You are in control of what responses and decisions you make in a storm. Sometimes it's unavoidable, but whenever and wherever possible, temporarily delay making crucial decisions in the midst of a storm. First, deal with the root cause of the storm as much as you can before making life-defining decisions.

We understand that there are times where the storm is directly affected by decisions that must be made on the spot. You might be in a combative argument with someone, but it's your decision as to whether the argument escalates to a more serious and dangerous place. Every argument or even conversational discussion is cultivating a decision. When you do have to make a decision in a storm, follow Jesus' example and speak to the source causing the storm while you're making the decisions. Whatever the seen "symptom" of the storm, the enemy is behind the things designed to separate you from God and His will. Release your voice in authority against the enemy and all his maneuvers and operations, and make it clear he must cease and desist. If you need to do so, keep reminding him he has been rendered powerless to continue any of his afflicting behaviors.

...and the waves beat into the ship, so that it was now full.

Mark 4:37 KJV

The word for "waves" means "to be pregnant, to swell, to bend, curve and billow as if bursting or toppling." These waves were causing all to lose their balance, equilibrium and focus.

The Amplified Bible says "the waves kept beating into the boat." The word for "beat" means "to superimpose, throw upon, stretch forth, to think upon." It carries the thought "to strike in continual waves with repeated, relentless blows." The word used here for "beat" always refers to a person or personality. Satan is the personality at work underlying all difficulties and at the root of opposition to the Word of

82

God and knowledge of God. Opposition to the will of God emanates from the primary opposition that the enemy has to all things of God.

So when we face persecution, pressure from people, take note that we're not wrestling against flesh and blood but against the hierarchies of hell and its residents. Many times people can just look at the physical circumstances and seek to only address the physical circumstances in a storm or crisis. *But one thing to keep in mind first is that you must understand and discover if there are spiritual conditions or spiritual influences that are the underlying causes of the problems you're facing.*

If you keep facing financial lack, and you just keep selling what you have or you just keep getting a second and third job, it may provide temporary relief but may never deal with the root issue driving the lack. And what will you do when you run out of things to sell and lack the energy and time to find a fourth or fifth job? Seek the counsel of God to understand the root cause for the repetition of lack or whatever adverse circumstances that keep appearing in your life from season to season. Until the root is dealt with appropriately, dealing with symptoms will only allow the problems to persist in the future.

It may be pre-conditioned beliefs and behaviors lodged within the heart, unconsciously repeated that keeps landing you in undesirable circumstances. If it is, find scripture that solves that issue. Fight a spiritual condition with a spiritual solution.

There's another tactic of the enemy called the "pile-on, pile-up" technique. Have you ever tried to carry too much stuff and end up dropping most of it, making a mess, getting frustrated, and prolonging a task that should have taken half the time? The enemy likes to stack activities and demands on your time and in your life to get you piled up so that you get frustrated, paralyzed, and ineffective in your activities.

When I was younger, I would play football with the neighborhood guys. Many times I would be the quarterback or ball carrier, and obviously, because of my position, I would be the object of every guy on the defenses' attention. I was pretty slippery when it came to getting tackled—I didn't like being hit and jumped on by several guys at a time.

Every once in a while, I would get tackled by four or five guys who would pile on top of me and hold me down for a bit before getting off me. As you can imagine in pick-up games at the park, we didn't have officials handing out penalties, so a little bit of everything went on. I can still remember how unpleasant it was to be at the bottom of the pile. For a brief moment, you feel like they'll never get up. You can't move, and it's hard to breathe and free your lungs to get that next breath of air. That was the "pile on, pile up" technique.

Have you ever felt like you were at the bottom of the pile? The pile is designed to come on you with one thing after another, like being beaten with repeated, relentless blows of a fist. Satan will try to pile on top of your life and hit you with wave after wave of afflictions—bills, bodily symptoms, relational problems, fears, doubts, worries, and seemingly hopeless situations. This tactic will bring waves of thoughts to think upon, and thoughts that seem to stretch out over your soul—your mind, will, emotions, and imaginations—to try and smother you like a weighted and water soaked canvas, to overwhelm, suffocate, and drown you with defeat, failure, and destructive outcomes.

If that happens to you, just know it's the pile up technique. It may seem like it'll last forever, but "this too shall pass." You'll get to the other side if you use the voice of authority. When you speak authoritatively affirming your faith and declared from scripture, it energizes your hope. You must continue in this way of imposing your will. It may initially seem that things aren't changing, but hold the line and stay the course. Glimmers of hope will emerge. What seems dark and hopeless will begin to become brightened and infused with an expectation that things are getting better and will continue to do so.

I know what it's like to face hardship, feel depressed, and almost resigned to life never getting better. I know what it's like to hear the taunts of the enemy in the ears of my soul telling me I will never be healed of some malady or another, of never having a better life than where I am presently situated at the time, of being condemned and tormented in the prison of a mind under siege. But I also know what it's like to come out on the other side, free of the sickness or injury, free of darkness and depression, free from the lies and deceptions of the enemy. Where I felt weighted down and sinking further away from what God promised, like the disciples, I was able to rise out of the sinking ship.

The boat the disciples were on began to fill with water to the point of sinking into the depths of the sea. Just like the wind created pregnant, swelling, bending, curving waves that sent water onto the deck of the boat, tough circumstances will try to whip up your emotions like waves to keep beating and putting pressure on your soul to the point that you feel overwhelmed and about to sink. This is the time when you must become the master over your circumstances. But in Mark 4, that wasn't the case with the disciples.

Because of their circumstances, their lives were now full of panic, fear, worry, and pressure. Circumstances can escalate emotions which in turn can escalate the circumstances. When this happens, a person is actually colluding against themselves to intensify negative feelings and bring defeat into their lives. Action has to be taken. Getting the Master involved is a good idea but not from the frame of mind and panic with which the disciples awakened Jesus.

When they alerted Jesus to what was happening on the boat, notice the contrast between Jesus and the disciples.

And He (Jesus) was in the hinder part of the ship,
asleep on a pillow: and they awake Him, and say unto
Him, Master, carest thou not that we perish?

Mark 4:38 KJV

While the disciples were in a panic, Jesus was asleep. This had to have been a deep sleep, because the storm was violent, the winds were whipping, the waves were crashing, the boat was filling with water, the disciples were shouting and crying out in panic. Sometimes, one of the best things you can do in the face of your problems is entrust them to the care of God and get to a place of rest. You might even need to go to sleep, but whatever you do, cast your cares upon Him!

The disciples shouted to Jesus, "We are sinking and about to drown! Don't you care that we're all about to perish?" One translation of the Bible interprets this verse, "Does it matter to you that we're going under and about to die?

Getting the Master involved so you can be master over your circumstances is indeed a good idea, the right and best idea. It's a great idea. It's a God idea. But how you approach Him is important. The disciples approached Jesus in fear and doubt. As hard as it can be, when we're in storms and crisis, we have to muster our spiritual strength and intestinal fortitude to remain in a place of faith and trust toward God, respecting Him for not only what you need and what He can do, but who He is and who He will be. Of course it matters to Him. Always stay on God's side. He'll help the one who cries out to Him. Cry out in faith and trust.

We've got to understand that their words of doubt were stout words in direct opposition to "Let us go over to the other side." No matter how dire the circumstances seem, remember His words, "I'll see you through this, I'll sustain you and uphold you, and you will make it through this just fine. Everything's going to be alright. Everything's going to be okay."

Studying Jesus' actions in the storm, we'll see the manner of action we are to take if we face hard, even dangerous times. Don't only read the words He spoke, but catch the spirit of what Jesus said and did.

> *And He arose, and rebuked the wind, and said unto the sea, Peace, be still. And the wind ceased, and there was a great calm.*
>
> *Mark 4:39 KJV*

Let's look at the contrasts once again, not to criticize or condemn the disciples, but to see and understand how to do this and experience what's possible.

To their credit, they did turn to Jesus in their time of need, but the disciples spoke to Jesus in panic about the problem. In contrast, Jesus rebuked the wind and spoke to the sea. They never spoke to the wind, the sea or themselves with the remembrance of and confidence in the word, "Let us pass over to the other side." They never spoke to themselves with the word Jesus taught that day and said just before leaving.

The disciples never dealt with the root and source of what caused the storm, nor did they consider the root cause and source reason of the storm itself. The root cause of the storm was found in the cursed nature of the earth—the wind over which they had authority to exercise. The specific root cause and source of the storm itself was the enemy opposing the Word, and Jesus' mission and assignment for crossing over to the other side of the sea.

The disciples said exclusively what they had and what they were experiencing. Jesus said what He wanted and desired both before the storm and during the storm. He spoke the expected outcome for the future and against the present circumstances. He called things that be not into existence, as if they already were in existence. He knew things were so, not just when He saw what He wanted to happen, but when He said what He wanted to happen.

Jesus commanded the outcome. Even when the circumstances came to oppose His words, His will and His authority, Jesus happened to the circumstances. The circumstances didn't just happen to Him. The disciples were doing everything they could to ride out and somehow survive the storm. Jesus initiated a change of events and altered the atmosphere around Him. The disciples felt no power or authority had been given to them to change things that were happening to them. The disciples regarded themselves as men subject to the laws of the earth. Jesus saw Himself as the one with dominion over the laws of the earth.

Even when the circumstances came to oppose His words, His will and His authority, Jesus happened to the circumstances, the circumstances didn't just happen to Him.

Let's investigate what Jesus did and the frame of thinking behind His words and actions. After being awakened, Jesus arose. Remember how the storm arose? Suddenly, violently, out of nowhere and with great vigor. The word for how Jesus "arose" from sleep is different from how the storm arose and means "to wake fully, raise and stir up."

As you trace the root of this word, it also means "to gather in the chief meeting place, town square, market, thoroughfare or street." It also has the idea of "collecting one's faculties to waken from sleep, from sitting or lying, from disease, from death, from obscurity or inactivity, to stand up, take up and arise from ruins."

In the midst of a storm or crisis, there are times when you need to have a "town square meeting" in the chief meeting place of your mind and decide from the Word of God what you want and how you want things and circumstances to be in your life. In a storm, you're going to have to fully awaken and collect your faculties to rise up out of whatever is trying to ruin your day, hinder you in a certain season of time, or handicap your life as a whole. You will have to use the voice of authority to possess what rightfully belongs to you and stand up to oppositional circumstances and against the enemy. Put your circumstances and the enemy in their place with your authoritative decrees and declarations.

Jesus rebuked the wind. The word for "rebuked" means "forbid, immediately charged, censured and admonished." It also means "(to place) a tax upon." The Bible says Jesus rebuked the wind, which doesn't necessarily mean Jesus said, "Wind, I rebuke you."

Have you ever been rebuked? Did the rebuker say, "John" or "Jane, I rebuke thee?" Probably not. How do you rebuke a person? A proper rebuke takes into account unmet requirements and points out behavior that's unacceptable. A rebuke then gives expectations of changing to an attitude or behavior that's acceptable and gives an expectation that things will change within a certain amount of time. An effective rebuke is very clear and accurate in what's being brought into account for resolution and change.

By understanding the meaning of the word "rebuke," I believe we can grasp the spirit of what Jesus said when He, "rebuked the wind." Following the rebuke of the wind, Jesus spoke to the sea, "Peace, be still." Jesus took and aimed words that enforced His rights based in God's word. What rights? We'll cover this in greater detail later, but there were several basic, legal, covenant rights from which Jesus operated that, among other things, included the authority of Adam,

Abraham, Mosaic Law, and David

Jesus rebuked and controlled the wind—the circumstances—out of the reservoir of dominion and governing power He had over His own will and soul. This allowed Him to specifically, purposefully and accurately target the release of authority through His words.

Jesus "said to the sea, Peace, be still." Jesus spoke the desired outcome from this place of dominion and legal authority. He ordered the chaos to be still. And He did this on the basis of the written Word of which He had an ingrained understanding.

The floods have lifted up, O Lord, the floods have lifted up their voice; the floods lift up their waves. The Lord on high is mightier than the noise of many waters, yea, than the mighty waves of the sea.

Psalm 93:3-4 KJV

Thou rulest the raging of the sea: when the waves thereof arise, Thou stillest them.

Psalm 89:9 KJV

Then they cry unto the Lord in their trouble, and He bringeth them out of their distresses. He maketh the storm a calm, so that the waves thereof are still. Then are they glad because they be quiet; so He bringeth them unto their desired haven.

Psalm 107:28-30 KJV

Jesus could stand with great confidence on the boat in the face of the storm and speak from His rights to "arise and still the raging sea and the waves." Even if a flood lifts up its voice, the voice of the Lord is like many waters and much greater in volume. His voice is higher and mightier than the noise of many waters and mightier than the mighty waves of the sea.

During the times when the cares of life and the roar of hardened circumstances seek to drown out the voice of the Lord, we can have confidence that His voice is mightier. Our rights and responsibilities are to cry out to the Lord, and then use our voice just as He would use His to make the storms calm so that the waves thereof are still and we are safely brought to our desired havens in life.

Operating effectively in the voice of authority will require you to diligently search the scriptures for what needs to be coming out of your mouth. It will require you to seek the sound of His voice in your spirit to know the word to speak in season. If you want to change the scenery in your life, you must change the sounds coming out of your mouth.

There are times you've got to make your life be still before you can see any change in your circumstances *or reach your desired haven.* You can still your life by speaking peace and calm into your soul, then into your circumstances. Whenever the world around you is swirling in confusion and chaos, you must command your soul to "be at ease", command your mind to "be still and be at peace."

The way circumstances appear in your life are connected to how you see them in your soul. Remember, we don't see things the way they are, we see things the way we are. The good news in all of this is that you can use the law of dominant images mentioned in chapter 3 to your advantage to pull you out of any undesired circumstances to build a new and better reality. Determine what that reality is. Once you determine the direction and reality you need or want your life to go in, make sure it's God's will and way and make it your strongest image in life.

Wrap your heart, mind, and words around the most pressing, urgent, and major needs in your life right now. Make the solution from the Word the most dominant image in your life, and make that solution the most dominant words coming out of your mouth.

The word Jesus used for "peace" to still the sea means "silence, hush." It carries the thought of "involuntary stillness or inability to speak." Once peace is in your soul, the circumstances can no longer speak to you or against you with any kind of demonstrated force that unsettles your soul and will. Once you make the windy chaos of circumstances to be still, they have no voluntary will to oppose you.

The word Jesus used for "still" means "muzzle." Your voice of authority muzzles the voices of opposition and can suppress the voice of the enemy. One moment the circumstances and the enemy may be screaming at you, but at your rebuke and command, they are muzzled into silence.

Then He arose and rebuked the wind, and said to the sea, Peace, be still! And the wind ceased and there was a great calm.

Mark 4:39 KJV

The results from accurately and effectively releasing the voice of authority caused the wind to cease and caused a great calm. "Ceased" means "to tire, relax, reduce in strength, to chop down or beat down." The Amplified Bible says, "And the wind ceased (sank to rest as if exhausted by its beating) and there was (immediately) a great calm (a perfect peacefulness).

There was a beat down that took place and it was Jesus beating down the circumstances and oppositions in His life by exerting His faith through the voice of authority against circumstances and opposition. The storm wore itself out and got beat down and there was a great and immediate calm. As greatly and suddenly as the storm arose, the same degree and immediacy of calm settled over the sea and was available to the disciples in the boat and the other little ships around them.

In an instance, other than a little water in the boat and some sea soaked clothes, it was as if the storm had never even arisen. It was as if it hadn't hit or existed. One moment it was one way, and in the next moment it was all changed! There are times in life where we may have sorrow that lasts for a night or a brief season, but there's joy and laughter that follows. Through the voice of authority, God can turn mourning into laughter and sorrow into joy. He can turn chaos into peace.

Let Him use your voice to enforce His will through your authority and some things you need to turnaround can happen suddenly. That's my decree to you and declaration over your life. Things that were one way will change suddenly as you release the voice of authority and stand on your own declarations in faith.

> *And He said unto them, Why are ye so fearful? How is it that ye have no faith? And they feared exceedingly, and said one to another, What manner of man is this, that even the wind and the sea obey Him?*
>
> *Mark 4:40–41 KJV*

Jesus' question to them was to say, "You heard this Word taught today, you heard My instructions. How come you got afraid and forgot what I said?" He expected them to do what He had just done to the storm. Luke's version of this account has the disciples saying that Jesus "commanded the wind and the sea." Jesus fully expected the disciples to do what He did. He expected that they, likewise, could have used their authority to voice commands which the wind and sea would have had to obey.

The disciples were instead left to wonder and question, "What manner of man is this?" The answer that Jesus was demonstrating on the boat and in the times that followed this incident was, "The manner of man I am is the same manner of man you are when you take your voice to speak My word and My will to release faith through your authority in the earth in agreement with heaven."

Are most people there yet? On the largest scale, no, they are not. But that's why we have to learn, know, study, and grow in our understanding and application of what Jesus was teaching about the voice of authority. We may make mistakes along the way, but no one ever learned much of anything afraid to make mistakes. It's what we do to learn from our mistakes, and not back down from what's rightfully ours, that will make the difference in our lives and in the lives of those around us.

This is a good thing for everybody to voice, but especially if you're facing difficulties and storms, make this declaration of faith over your life in your voice of authority (it would do you well to define the specific circumstances you desire to see changed):

"Circumstances of my life, I'm speaking to you.

Circumstances and storms in my life, I command you to stop your chaos and confusion, and be at peace. I command you, confusion, leave my life, my home, my relationships, my finances, my ministry and my work. I say, "Peace, be still." Soul, be at peace, be at ease. I call clarity of vision and purpose to me now. I call wisdom and favor to me now. Spirit of truth, lead me into all truth, show me things to come. Spirit of Grace, come upon me, to live what truth requires, and to do what truth commands.

In many respects, spiritually speaking, we need to be like a good laboratory scientist. We need to be like spiritual scientists constantly exercising our understanding, not being offended or discouraged by seeming failures along the way to growing in our expertise, to use the voice of authority.

One thing that helped Jesus to function the way He did was His knowing the authority that was rightfully His to use and why. Let's further explore structural knowledge that will help us to access our authority and put added confidence, boldness, and results in the voice with which we speak in the earth.

Chapter 5

The Authority Jesus Accessed in the Earth

While in the earth, Jesus operated in His rights based on the authority of each of the covenants God made throughout His dealings with man, from Adam's time in Eden to the time of King David. This included the Edenic covenant and the dominion God gave man, the Adamic covenant with its promise of a redeemer, and the Noahic, Abrahamic, Mosaic, Palestinian, and Davidic covenants. Before we look briefly at each of these seven covenants and the authority they granted man in the earth, and also the New Covenant, let's consider the definition of covenant.

God initiated covenants with the purpose of establishing His will in the earth, to set up an enduring relationship with man and to enhance the quality of life man would have in the earth. The ultimate intent of all the biblical covenants mentioned was originally to point us to Jesus.

Throughout human history and in modern times, covenants have been entered into for three primary reasons. Two of the three reasons are for business and for protection. But the most prominent reason for covenant, is love, as illustrated in the marriage covenant. Covenants of love establish an enduring sense of commitment and lifelong intimacy of relationship. And covenants of love are designed to ingrain the strongest reality of authority between covenant partners.

The English word "covenant" means a mutual understanding between two or more individuals or groups, each binding him or herself to fulfill specified obligations; a legal contract; a binding agreement; a written agreement; a solemn agreement listing specific things to do or not to do; to share mutually in any assets or debts and to mutually protect and defend each other.

The Hebrew word for covenant is "berith" and means a compact or agreement which signals the "cutting of covenant," indicating that there was a cutting in the flesh to where the blood flows from the body. It also means a compact or agreement made by passing between pieces of flesh and walking through blood. When a covenant was being agreed upon, an animal would be cut in half and the two individuals or group representatives entering covenant would walk between the pieces of the animal in a figure eight pronouncing terms of the covenant, and the blessings and curses of the covenant.

In the New Testament, there are two Greek words for covenant: *diatheke* and *suntithemai*, but we'll focus only on the first word listed here. *Diatheke* means a disposition, arrangement, testament or will; a will that has been ratified and approved; a declaration of purpose or the declaration of one person's will; an arrangement that has been made by one individual or group who possesses plenary power, which the receiving individual or group may accept or reject, but they cannot alter the arrangements presented in a way that makes the original arrangements take on different meanings or conditions.

As a disposition, covenant means "a final, orderly arrangement or settlement and the transfer of title, authority, privilege or possessions to the care or ownership of another." In relation to covenant, the word plenary means "to be complete in every respect; absolute; unqualified; full."

In this context, we can note that God has plenary power. God has power that is complete in every respect, absolute, unqualified—meaning that no one can call His qualifications into question. He has the power to transfer authority and possessions into the care or ownership of another. In every covenant, God presented a final, orderly arrangement that transferred a title, authority, privilege, and possessions to the stewardship of a man or group. This means God had the unqualified and uncontested right to give man full and unhindered access to His will in the earth. God was making all of His assets available to man. God committed to protect and defend every man that was in covenant with Him.

As the initiator of covenant, God uses plenary power to present arrangements that can only be accepted or rejected, but where man cannot alter or change any of the original meanings or conditions of covenant arrangements as presented by God. Paul highlighted the unchangeable nature of covenant in writing to the Galatians, explaining how men who make covenants among themselves consider that a covenant, once entered, cannot be changed, altered, added to, or taken away from.

> *Brethren, I speak in the manner of men: though it is only a man's covenant, yet if it is confirmed, no one annuls or adds to it.*
>
> *Galatians 3:15 NKJV*

Paul's point is that this wasn't just an agreement between men but between God and man and between God and Jesus. God gave the promise in the covenant to a man and His descendants, and nothing can annul, make void, or cancel a covenant promise that comes from God.

> *Now to Abraham and his Seed were the promises made, He does not say, "And to seeds," as of many, but as of one, "And to your Seed," who is Christ. And this I say, that the law, which was four hundred and thirty years later, cannot annul the covenant that was confirmed before by God in Christ, that it should make*

the promise of no effect. For if the inheritance is of the law, it is no longer of promise, but God gave it to Abraham by promise.

Galatians 3:16–18 NKJV

Anything God promises is revealing His will. His promises are certain and sure. Knowing His will is a matter of knowing what He's said to man in covenant. The enemy may challenge our willingness to speak, act, and expect with authority, but when we know the guarantees, promises, and assurances of covenant, we can release our voice with unchallenged rights of authority. Let's go through a few highlights of the covenants that impacted Jesus' authority in the earth.

The Edenic Covenant

The Edenic covenant was originally given by virtue of Creation and was meant to be extended to all humanity by birthright into the human race. Genesis 1:26-28 says "And God said, Let us make man in our image, after our likeness: and let them have dominion…

So God created man in his own image, in the image of God created He him; male and female created He them. And God blessed them, and God said unto them, Be fruitful, and multiply, and replenish the earth, and subdue and have dominion (in the earth)."

This was the command God gave Adam upon creation. This was God's original plan for man and provided ten things to benefit man. Several of these things included the fact that God formed the earth for man so that it would be inhabited and enjoyed by man, that man was the focal point of God's creation, that God revealed His purpose for man, that God made man in His image and likeness, that man was blessed by God, and given the commands to be fruitful, multiply, replenish the earth, subdue the earth, and have dominion in the earth.

His original plan was resumed through Jesus as the son of Adam, who was the son of God. The authority of the Edenic covenant was available to Jesus by virtue of birthright into the human race. Notice also from the stated lineage of Jesus that His family roots trace back through David, Abraham, and Noah as well.

> *Now Jesus Himself began His ministry at about thirty years of age, being (as was supposed) the son of Joseph.*
>
> *Luke 3:23 NKJV*

Time passed does not alter a covenant. The family bloodlines establish a continuity to covenant. Jesus was able to trace his natural bloodline back to Adam and ultimately to the covenant authority given to Adam as the son of God.

...which was the son of David... Which was the son of Jacob, which was the son Isaac, which was the son of Abraham, ...which was the son of Noah...which was the son of Adam, which was the son of God.

Luke 3:31, 34, 36, 38 KJV

The bloodline of a person determines the nature and privileges of a person. In being born of a virgin with God being His Father, Jesus inherited the same image at birth that Adam had when he was formed by God, but without the taint of sin that came at the fall of man. In the Gospels, Jesus frequently referred to himself as the son of man. This son of man also retained family rights and sonship lineage all the way back through David, Joseph, Jacob, Isaac, Abraham, Noah, Adam, and, ultimately, God.

And so it is written, "The first man Adam was made a living being." The last Adam was made a life-giving spirit.

1 Corinthians 15:45

The last Adam, Jesus, became the firstborn from the dead and the first of a new creation or new spiritual species of beings. When we accept Christ, we become born again family members in this new species of beings. We automatically assume the full family rights and sonship lineage in the same manner as Jesus had in the earth, and we have the same rights and authority He has now as the one legally seated in heavenly places at the right hand of the Father. We'll go a little further into these new covenant rights and authority later, but suffice it to say that we have greater authority than we've accessed to this time in history.

As a son of Adam and as the son of God, Jesus effectively used his God-given dominion over the earth to command the wind to obey His voice. The manner of man Jesus was in the earth is the manner of man we are authorized to be in the earth today. We must learn how to use this authorization. Many people become frustrated because they never learn and grow into their place of authority. They attempt an act of authority and seem to fail and assume that it must not be true.

Again, we need to have as much sense as a good laboratory scientist. Just because one experiment or endeavor doesn't produce a perfected result, we don't give up on the pursuit of a cure or an answer. Keep plugging away, diligently seeking the right proportions or right methods.

We must not stop our training because of a roadblock or seeming failure. We must be trained in this manner of man we are. We must practice and exercise the voice of authority. We must deliberately and intentionally release the voice of authority and assume the supernatural nature within us. And the time to do so is now.

The Adamic Covenant

With the fall of man through the sin of Adam, there was another key authority Jesus was given access to through the Adamic covenant. The Adamic covenant is the covenant God initiated with Adam and Eve in the Garden of Eden after the fall of man and the entrance of sin into man's history. God declared His divine intent and purpose to bring a complete redemption of man through the redeemer to come hundreds of years in the future. In Genesis 3:15, God pronounced judgment upon the serpent, Satan, and promised redemption for man through Jesus, man's Savior.

And I will put enmity between you and the woman, and between your seed and her Seed; He shall bruise your head and you shall bruise His heel.

Genesis 3:15 NKJV

One very important trait to understand about God is that He is solution oriented. As soon as man rebelled and committed an act of treason against God, He began the process of restoration to redeem man back to all he lost. The mercy and grace of God is amazing. Covenant is revelation of authority made available, but it's also the unlimited expression of mercy and grace, the crowning reality of unconditional love. Love prepares answers ahead of the time of need. That heart to prepare is at the heart of covenant.

In the case of God's man in the Garden, God has just seemingly lost the crown of His creation. It appears that His plan to have a family has resulted in abject failure. It looked like God's enemy had stolen His prized creation and taken over the authority of the earth. What was God's response? His response was the immediate and full enactment of a plan of redemption. That's how God thinks, acts, speaks, and lives. That's how we likewise should be in the face of seeming defeats.

Through the rights of the Adamic covenant, Jesus accepted, walked in and lived in the responsibility and authority to be man's Redeemer. Jesus was bruised for our healing and redemption, and God endorsed and fulfilled Jesus' authority to bruise the head of the serpent, to defeat and spoil the enemy's kingdom and to render Satan's power to be ineffective against the man or woman who would accept and cooperate with the finished work of Christ as redeemer.

Knowing that you were not redeemed with corruptible things, like silver or gold, from your aimless conduct received by tradition from your fathers, But with the precious blood of Christ, as of a lamb without blemish and without spot.

1 Peter 1:18-19 NKJV

The evidence of our redemption is the blood of Jesus.

The life of the flesh is in the blood, and because covenant is representative of the life of the covenant makers, covenant requires blood as the payment and assurance price. Life is represented and contained within the blood. We're redeemed by the life in the blood of Jesus. Because covenant is sealed in blood, His blood has given us His life by covenant.

The Noahic Covenant

God made the Noahic covenant with Noah and his sons after the flood, involving all living creatures and all future generations of mankind upon the face of the earth. This covenant promised continued favor and protection from natural disasters on Noah, his family, and their descendants and invoked continued rights for man to be fruitful and multiply throughout the earth.

> *... Then the Lord said in His heart, "I will never again curse the ground for man's sake...nor will I again destroy every living thing as I have done. While the earth remains, seedtime and harvest, cold and heat, winter and summer, and day and night shall not cease.*
>
> *Genesis 8:21-22 NKJV*

Notice the on-going reality of seedtime and harvest shall not cease as long as the earth remains. Seedtime and harvest is listed as enduring right along with temperature changes, seasonal changes and, the calendar progressing through day and night changes.

By covenant, God promised that every seed must grow and increase into a harvestable state. That's God's part. Every harvest must be brought in. That's man's part. Many people assume that if they plant a seed, the harvest is automatic. Believing a harvest is automatically enjoyed would be like a farmer expecting a corn harvest to march into a storage site and into neatly packed sacks on its own once it's ripened to maturity.

In a covenant between God and man, man has the responsibility to plant seed and harvest the crop. God has the responsibility of protecting the seed sown and growing and maturing the harvest. This is a simplification of the process, but when we do our part, the blessings of the covenant are experienced.

Remember, Jesus said that the sower sows the Word. So when the Word is sown in respect to covenant rights, we have the authority to expect a harvest on our words. When we speak words in the voice of authority, we can expect to harvest the content of those words in our lives.

So God blessed Noah and his sons, and said to them: Be fruitful and multiply, and fill the earth. And the fear of you and the dread of you shall be on every beast of the earth, on every bird of the air, on all that move on the earth, and on all the fish of the sea. They are given into your hand. And as for you, be fruitful and multiply;

bring forth abundantly in the earth, and multiply in it. Then God spoke to Noah and to his sons with him, saying, And as for Me, behold, I establish My covenant with you and with your descendants after you. Thus I establish My covenant with you: Never again shall all flesh be cut off by the waters of the flood; never again shall there be a flood to destroy the earth.

Genesis 9:1-2, 7-9, 11 NKJV

Always remember, the promise was given that seedtime and harvest would never cease as long as the earth remained. There would always be a means for provision and prosperity through this promise. They were given the responsibility and charge to be fruitful and replenish the earth. And God promised that there would be no further earth wide floods that would endanger and destroy all mankind.

Every time rains, hurricanes, tsunamis, and floods whip up in the earth, the enemy is trying to challenge and oppose God's covenant promise that floods will never again destroy the planet as it did in Noah's day. On the boat in Mark 4, to a lesser degree this storm was a direct challenge to God's covenant to Noah and his descendants. The enemy was attempting to use a windstorm to create destruction through waters flooding the boat. Jesus engaged the principle and authority of this covenant to defeat the challenge, and to command the winds to cease and the seas to be still.

In the Noahic covenant, God restored and reinstated

His purposes for the human race that had been threatened by the wickedness of man's heart. He sealed His covenant word with the guarantee of the rainbow as the sign of His faithfulness to His word for every generation.

> *And God said: "This is the sign of the covenant which I make between Me and you, and every living creature that is with you for perpetual generations. I set My rainbow in the cloud, and it shall be for the sign of the covenant between Me and the earth. It shall be, when I bring a cloud over the earth, that the rainbow shall be seen in the cloud. And I will remember My covenant which is between Me and you and every living creature of all flesh; the waters shall never again become a flood to destroy all flesh. The rainbow shall be in the cloud and I will look on it to remember the everlasting covenant between every living creature of all flesh that is on the earth." And God said to Noah, "This is the sign of the covenant which I have established between Me and all flesh that is on the earth."*
>
> *Genesis 9:12-17 NKJV*

This was not only a promise that Jesus had available, but one that we today can be mindful of every time we see a rainbow. And notice this, that God said He would Himself personally look at every rainbow and always remember the everlasting nature of His covenant with man. God has promised to never allow the floods of life to overtake and consume us. Life floods may come, but God raises up a standard to refute those floods as we take up our part in authority exercised in word and deed. He has established a system whereby we can always sow seed on every level and see it grow into a multiplied harvest that plentifully supplies and replenishes our every need.

Because seedtime and harvest is a law based on covenant, we have the authority and right to speak words that function as seed to produce after their kind. What we put in our words as a regular way of life is essential to understanding the types of things we harvest in life over time.

God has put a covenant principle of everlasting quality in our hands and within the scope of our authority. Our voice releases that authority. God enforces that authority and brings to pass every word we speak in agreement with any promise of covenant He has presented. He also protects our right to speak in opposition to what He's promised. It's unwise to speak against the promises of God, but the truth remains that words of contradiction and opposition also have a life in them to produce after their kind and produce a harvest in a person's life over time. On which side of the promise are your words?

The Abrahamic Covenant

Not only did Jesus operate in the authority of Eden's covenant of blessing, and the Adamic and Noahic covenant, but He also wielded the authority of Abraham. This authority, as well as the privileges and expectations of this covenant, were explained to Abraham in Genesis 12, 15, 17, and 22 and then elaborated upon further in later covenants. Let's look at these passages in Genesis.

> *Now the Lord had said to Abram, "Get out of your country, from your family and from your father's house, to a land that I will show you. I will make you a great nation; I will bless you, and make your name great; and you shall be a blessing. I will bless those who bless you, and I will curse him who curses you; and in you all the families of the earth shall be blessed."*
>
> *Genesis 12:1-3 NKJV*

In Genesis 12, God was introducing Himself to Abram. God was letting him know that He had great plans for him, that his future was connected to God and that if he accepted God's proposal, Abram's legacy and greatness would be forever sealed and enduringly stamped upon every generation of humanity to come. This is the kind of reality that God proposes to everyone who accepts the invitation into His family.

> *After these things the word of the Lord came to Abram in a vision, saying, "Do not be afraid, Abram. I am your shield, and your exceedingly great reward."*
>
> *Genesis 15:1 NKJV*

The latter part of Genesis 15 describes the actual "cutting of the covenant" that gave Abram the official authority to stand on the covenant promises God made in Genesis 12. During the years and events between Genesis 12 and 15, God engaged in covenant dialogue and demonstrated what it would mean to fully accept and enter the legally binding effects of the covenant. God repeatedly directed, protected, and prospered Abram and his family. This instilled confidence in Abram about the power, ability, willingness, and faithfulness of God.

In Genesis 15:1, God gives Abram His word and reinforces the security and assurance that He would protect Abram and be a great and immeasurable reward to Abram for his accepting and living in the covenant. In the context of the conversation with God, Abram asks God about an heir for his posterity. In Genesis 13, God had promised to give a great parcel of land to Abram and his descendants. At this point in Genesis 15, Abram has no offspring of his own and one not born of his body was being groomed to be the heir of all he had—which would include the land to come. God promises him that he would have a child with his wife, Sarai, and that his heir would be his offspring.

And behold, the word of the Lord came to him, saying, "This one shall not be your heir, but one who will come from your own body shall be your heir." Then He brought him outside and said, "Look now toward heaven, and count the stars if you are able to number them." And He said to him, "So shall your descendants be."

Genesis 15:4-5 NKJV

God promises Abram that his descendants would be multiplied like the stars of the sky. In doing this, God gave Abram another image to build within his heart and mind. This meant that whenever he saw the sand during the day and stars during the night, Abram would be reminded of the promise of God, and God would be building the dominant image of His promise within Abram.

To guarantee the legitimacy of the promises of Genesis 12, that Abram would be given an heir, descendants, land, the blessing and be used to usher in the redemption of all mankind through the Messiah, God offers Abram the opportunity to enter covenant with Him, and Abram accepts. And that very same day as recorded in **Genesis 15** they cut the covenant that established God's right to use Abram's family to give birth to the Messiah and to do all that God promised to Abram. And at the same time, God gave Abram the right to use His Family name and His Family authority in the earth.

On the same day, the Lord made a covenant with Abram, saying, To your descendants I have given this land...

Genesis 15:18 NKJV

God established covenant as the greatest place of authority. All authority originates with God and flows out of covenant agreements. God established a covenant with Adam in the Garden of Eden. God established a covenant with Noah coming out of the ark after the flood. And here in Genesis 15, God initiates and enters covenant with Abram to have authority expressed through Abram's family to influence events in the earth. This covenant would give a notable authority to Abram's family and those who come under the covenant to alter the course of history in the earth. Every covenant is God and man working together in joint authority to fulfill God's plans in the earth.

When Abram was ninety-nine years old, the Lord appeared to Abram and said to him, "I am Almighty God; walk before Me and be blameless. And I will make My covenant between Me and you and will multiply you exceedingly." Then Abram fell on his face, and God talked with him, saying: "As for Me, behold, My covenant is with you, and you shall be a father of many nations. No longer shall your name be called Abram, but your name shall be Abraham, for I have made you a father of many nations. I will make you exceedingly fruitful; and I will make nations of you, and kings shall come from you. And I will establish My covenant between Me and you and your descendants after you in their generations, for an everlasting covenant, to be God to you and your descendants after you. Also I give to you and your descendants after you the land

in which you are a stranger, all the land of Canaan,
as an everlasting possession; and I will be their God."
And God said to Abraham: "As for you, you shall keep
My covenant, you and your descendants after you
throughout their generations."

Genesis 17:1-9 NKJV

Decades had passed since the covenant was originally cut, and many events had taken place. One of those events was Abram fathering a child with his wife's handmaid, Hagar. It was done at the request of Abram's wife, Sarai, and resulted in the birth of Ishmael. Abram was 86 when Ishmael was born, and 13 years later God appeared here in Genesis 17 to talk to Abram about their covenant.

Abram hadn't walked entirely blameless before God in terms of covenant and had resigned himself to Ishmael being his heir. He probably thought, "God promised my heir would come from my body, and Ishmael is from my body." Although God promised to bless Ishmael and his descendants, Ismael wasn't the fulfillment of the promise given to Abram in the covenant.

In Genesis 17, God is reminding and correcting Abram. He also changed his name to Abraham, which had the meaning, "the father of many nations." God was not only changing his name but changing and re-directing Abraham's authority in the earth. God was using the voice of authority to "call those things which do not exist as though they did."

118

Learning to "call things that be not as though they are" is an important action to regularly use for those who would use the voice of authority in the earth.

The voice of authority is empowered to alter circumstances by hearing words from God, either from what's written in the scriptures or from what's spoken in our hearts that line up with what's written. We take and speak these words to change the appearance of things seen. Whatever we have in life that is undesired and opposes what God says can be changed. The undesired thing is a temporary reality that will conform to the enduring, eternal reality of God's word. We take and speak what God says so that we may bring to pass the things that agree with the desires we have that line up with God's will.

> *(As it is written, "I have made you [referring to Abraham] a father of many nations) in the presence of Him whom He believed–God, who gives life to the dead and calls those things which do not exist as though they did.*
>
> *Romans 4:17 NKJV*

Armed with the voice of authority, we speak of the desired thing that does not yet physically exist as though it has already appeared. This is exactly what God did in redefining Abram's reality as though it already were so. When we say the name, Abraham, we think of the man's name, what he answered by when someone wanted to get his attention. When God spoke it, and when Abraham heard it, he was hearing, "father of many nations."

This was a new privilege, a new level of authority, a new reality for him. It was designed to instill a new image, an image to dominate his thinking, bolster his believing, strengthen his expectations, influence how he spoke, and elevate his way of life. Every time someone spoke his name, he didn't just hear sounds that identified him so another person could speak with him. He heard an inspired word revealed from God. He heard a promise and reality from God. He heard the future of his family. He heard a covenant that authorized him to live out the image God had been putting in him every time he saw the sand and stars, or heard his name, Abraham.

He heard the things necessary to strengthen him to pass the greatest test of his life that would come in being told to offer as a sacrifice his only son and the child God promised to him, Isaac. When God told Abraham to give Isaac on the altar, Abraham acted immediately without hesitation. How could he do this? The only way Abraham could move on what God said was by understanding his authority in covenant with God and by relying upon the faithfulness of God, his covenant partner.

From the moment Abraham heard the instructions, he had to have reflected and meditated upon the history between him and God, and the only conclusion Abraham could come to was that God knew His business and would uphold His side of the covenant if he did his part. Abraham's faith and trust in God was once again rewarded when God provided Himself a sacrifice to substitute for Isaac.

> *Then the Angel of the Lord called to Abraham a second time out of heaven, And said: "By Myself I have sworn, says the Lord, because you have done this thing, and have not withheld your son, your only son—Blessing I will bless you, and multiplying I will multiply your descendants as the stars of the heaven and as the sand which is on the seashore; and your descendants shall possess the gate of their enemies. In your seed all the nations of the earth shall be blessed, because you have obeyed My voice."*
>
> *Genesis 22:15-18 NKJV*

Gate was symbolic of the strength and authority of a people. In a natural sense, later generations of Israelites who stayed under the authority of the Abrahamic covenant defeated the enemies in the land God had given to them. Generations later, Jesus made a statement found in Matthew 16:18, that "the gates of hell would not prevail against the church." This wasn't referring to the church or God's called out people, holding on for dear life while hell bombarded the church. It meant that the enemy's strongholds would not be able to withstand or resist the bombardments of the new creation man or woman in the heavens or on the earth.

When you think back on the story we've looked at from Mark 4, Jesus understood and operated in this authority against the source of the storms to take control of the land, and the air over the land that was given to Abraham and his descendants. The storm could not prevail against the authority Jesus exerted. That's why I say that the circumstances didn't just happen to Jesus, but Jesus happened to the circumstances.

But there's another very important authority that Jesus would have drawn from Abraham's encounter with God in Genesis 22 that we need to notice. Abraham offered his only son, Isaac, on the altar. Isaac is called his "only son" because he was the only son of his marriage covenant with Sarah, and Isaac was the only son of promise through covenant from God.

By faith Abraham, when he was tried, offered up Isaac: and he that had received the promises offered up his only begotten son, Of whom it was said, That in Isaac shall thy seed be called: Accounting that God was able to raise him up, even from the dead; from whence also he received him in a figure.

Hebrews 11:17-19 KJV

Even though he didn't have to physically go through with the act, Abraham had already fully committed the act in his heart in the presence of God. And Abraham had so completely taken on the nature of God through his covenant authority that he had received Isaac in a figure—in an image—as raised from the dead after giving him as a sacrifice. This was Abraham "giving life to the dead and calling those things which do not exist as though they did."

In fact, Abraham's faith is the first recorded incidence of someone potentially being raised from the dead in the scriptures. Where would Abraham get the faith to believe for the resurrection of a dead person? From God's promise that in Isaac would his seed be called. He got the faith for this from the covenant and God's faithfulness in the past, and Abraham released his rights and authority for it concluding and accounting that God was able, God was willing and God would have to raise up Isaac if He was going to fulfill the promise of the covenant.

Now get this: Abraham's faith to offer his only begotten son, Isaac, and his authority to expect Isaac to be raised from the dead is what allowed God to release faith and authority in the earth for His only begotten Son, Jesus, to be raised from the dead. The actions of one covenant partner made the promise come alive for the other covenant partner. When Abraham "received him (Isaac) in a figure," it legally authorized God to receive Jesus in a figure. The reality of the image begins in the heart and once it's ingrained in the heart, the physical expression is guaranteed to come to pass by continuing in the authority supported by covenant.

Jesus knew and understood this process and the authority necessary to be released through His voice for His resurrection. Remember, Jesus had received the commandment that allowed Him to lay His life down and to pick His life back up again. This commandment built an image within Jesus where He could see Himself in a "figure" raised from the dead. In remembering the story of Abraham being led to offer Isaac as a sacrifice, we can understand how this transaction between God and Abraham fit within the Abrahamic covenant. We can also see how the resurrection commandment and resultant authority would have instilled confidence in Jesus to be raised from the dead.

In the next chapter, we'll look at the impact the Mosaic, Palestinian, and Davidic covenants had on Jesus' operation of authority while He was here in the earth. We'll also peer into the basics of the New Covenant and have greater comprehension of it through understanding these previous covenants. All of them were leading up to the redemption of man and uncovering significant details about the New Covenant by which we operate with authority in the earth today. Each of these earlier covenants reveal some of the foundations upon which our New Covenant authority is built. When we better understand these foundations, the base of our authority is stronger, and the stronger our base, the further the reach and effectiveness of our voice of authority.

Chapter 6

Authority Concealed
and Revealed

The same way an intelligent inhabitant of any country might study the laws that provide benefits to citizens of that country, Jesus studied the Word, and correspondingly the covenants, to understand His authority to claim His benefits. He lived and operated like a citizen of the kingdom of God, and like a citizen with a comprehensive understanding of the covenants.

Things can be concealed to the untrained eye, but the one who has a trained and exercised eye will see and experience things others don't see. Because Jesus had "seeing eyes" and "hearing ears" trained by the Lord, He staked claims to His rights by knowing the laws of the covenant. He exercised His authority and voiced His rights on the basis of the covenants.

In the Mosaic, Palestinian, and Davidic covenants we gain important understanding about Jesus' views on specific rights that were His in the land given to Abraham and his descendants. By learning like Jesus learned, we can become expertly skilled at walking in the land God's given us with visible results based on consistently releasing the voice of authority.

The Mosaic Covenant

God made the Mosaic covenant at Mount Sinai with Israel after the 430 years they spent in Egypt and just after the exodus from Egypt.

Now therefore if you will indeed obey My voice and keep My covenant, then you shall be a special treasure to Me above all people; for all the earth is Mine.

Exodus 19:5 NKJV

The Mosaic covenant introduced the ten commandments, the priesthood and its structure, the law, and the blood sacrifices as a systematic ritual to follow. This covenant was set up to be a tutor or schoolmaster to bring Israel and ultimately the world to faith in Jesus Christ as Savior of all.

The Mosaic covenant gave laws that were to govern Israel in three areas: the moral law, the civil law and the ceremonial law. The moral law was made up of the ten commandments and served as the measure and standard of righteousness and morality. Jesus fulfilled these and qualified Himself to access the benefits promised through keeping the commandments.

The civil law was comprised of numerous, specific

regulations that at heart were supposed to expand the fundamental principles of conduct contained in the moral law. These laws were practical applications on how to govern and live life in every area of daily life.

One reason these laws listed in the covenant were so important is that they contained clear guidelines that governed things like sanitation and hygiene. In modern times, we are accustomed to things addressed in the Mosaic covenant being regular services or protocols, but before these things were normal for a civilized society, God provided the information necessary to promote national health. Israel was set apart from other nations because they knew by God's laws how to properly handle things like garbage or waste, sickness, mold, and the dead.

While the other nations experienced shortened life spans because of immorality, unsanitary conditions, and not understanding the harm germs caused, God gave Israel practical laws to support the moral laws, and together these laws lengthened the life span of the Israelites and enhanced the quality of their lives. The problem came into play when they made these civil laws the centerpiece of what they thought it was to be close to God. They made washing their hands, washing pots properly and tithing on herbs more important than the ceremonial laws and their deeper meaning.

It was the ceremonial law that had to be maintained to

satisfy the spiritual life of Israel. The ceremonial laws were highly organized, highly detailed, and highly defined laws that were to govern a person's spiritual life and spiritual well-being. How to perform sacrifices, conduct festivals and respect feasts, how to present acceptable offerings to God to atone for the sins of the people and the nation were all covered in the ceremonial law

The Mosaic covenant revealed and established the Sanctuary of the covenant, referred to as the tabernacle in the wilderness. This is where the five offerings—the burnt offering, meal offering, peace offering, sin offering, and trespass offering—were to be performed by the priesthood in the Outer Court of the tabernacle. The purpose for the tabernacle was stated in Exodus 25:8.

And let them make Me a sanctuary, that I may dwell among them.

Exodus 25:8 NKJV

In keeping the covenant and respecting the integrity of the sanctuary, Israel would be keeping the dwelling of God among the people. Jesus understood this and operated in the authority contained in the Mosaic covenant to perfection. In doing so, He was the living embodiment of the presence of God wherever He walked.

You remember Jesus said that He didn't come to destroy the law, but rather that He came to fulfill the law. The Mosaic covenant was a revelation of the laws representative of the order of God. God gave the Mosaic covenant to highlight divine standards of righteousness. Man's own barometer of morality was insufficiently equipped to accurately, consistently, and justly define sin. By perfectly keeping the law, Jesus perfectly defeated sin.

The Mosaic covenant, or Mosaic Law, was given to reveal the need for an internal change in the nature of man by imposing external laws. These laws posted road signs for how to live an upright life, but were also to help develop an understanding that apart from a changed nature, man couldn't live up to the standards of God.

God's purpose wasn't just to see if we could jump over the bar of righteousness to His satisfaction. His purpose was so that He could not only dwell among men, but live within men. We know that the law couldn't give eternal life. That is, the law in and of itself didn't have the power to change the sin nature. The law basically could only curb the nature and desire to sin, and illustrated the fact that all had sinned and fallen short of the glory of God. Only the perfect sacrifice could make it possible to exchange the sin nature for righteousness through a covenant sealed in sinless blood. That's essentially what Jesus did in dying on the cross and paying the price for sin.

All of the sacrifices of the Mosaic covenant each pointed to the Redeemer that was coming. The sacrifices were designed in part to ingrain in the social conscience of Israel the need for a savior. The sacrifices were a daily and generational ritual so that when Jesus arrived they would recognize Him as the Lamb of God that takes away the sin of the world. Unfortunately, national Israel, for the most part, missed this point of the Mosaic covenant.

The Mosaic covenant was given to demonstrate the difference between grace and law. It was put in place to reveal to humanity as a whole that justification, or being made to be in right standing with God, comes not by observance of a set of rules and laws but is obtained by grace through faith as the gift of God. This revelation of grace would come through the redeemer and savior, Jesus Christ. And the revelation that grace is greater than law is to be received and partaken of by everyone who accepts Jesus' finished work.

And of His fullness we have all received, and grace for grace. For the law was given through Moses, but grace and truth came through Jesus Christ.

John 1:16-17 NKJV

The authority of the Mosaic covenant is found in the fulfillment of the law. Jesus perfectly fulfilled the law as the only human being to perfectly pass the law test. Jesus completed every "jot and every tittle" of the law with a perfect passing score. This externally authorized Jesus as the sinless, spotless Lamb of God. Jesus was born with the internal nature of God, and His perfect completion of the law validated His claims to pay for the price of sin for all mankind.

It's kind of like this: in sports, you may have two teams that are scheduled to play, but one team is undefeated in their record after playing all the best teams in their league. The other team is winless after playing all the worst teams in their league. On paper, there is no question who should win the game between the best team and the worst team. But they still have to play the game. They don't just award the victory on the basis of previous records.

As God, Jesus had all the reports of being the undefeated champion. When He became man—and was still perfectly God—He had to "play the game" and live His life in fulfilling the law as proof of His superiority over the law. And He did it after having taken on the nature of man. Jesus took man's previously winless record against the sin nature and turned it around to become the undefeated champion for man.

For He made Him who knew no sin to be sin for us, that we might become the righteousness of God in Him.

2 Corinthians 5:21 NKJV

Another way to think of it is that Jesus took our failing grade in exchange for His passing grade so He could pay the price for our failure in sin. Jesus knew no sin, no defeat or failure, and took our sin nature and became sin for us. He exchanged our sin nature for His righteousness nature so we could experience the liberty of redemption and be born again with the nature of God.

By "coming in the likeness of men, and being found in appearance as a man," as Philippians 2:7-8 says, Jesus became a partaker of flesh and blood.

Inasmuch then as the children have partaken of flesh and blood, He Himself likewise shared in the same, that through death He might destroy him who had the power of death, that is, the devil, And release those who through fear of death were all their lifetime subject to bondage.

Hebrews 2:14-15 NKJV

What this means is that Jesus was qualified and authorized to pay the price for sin IF He fulfilled the law from a nature free of sin. Then all He had to do was literally pay the price—the wages—of sin. Romans 6:23 says "The wages of sin is death, but the gift of God is eternal life in Christ Jesus our Lord."

I don't mean to make this payment sound trivial, because it was a grievous price to pay. But pay it He did and now any man, woman, or child who believes and accepts this work Jesus has already performed to its completion and perfection can have eternal life as the free gift of God. It also means the one who believes and accepts this work can operate in the full authority Jesus acquired in and through the Mosaic covenant.

The Palestinian Covenant

God made the Palestinian covenant with the second generation of Israelites who had left Egypt but had been dwelling in the wilderness for 40 years. This covenant was established while they were in the land of Moab just prior to entering into the promised land of the Abrahamic covenant.

> *These are the words of the covenant which the Lord commanded Moses to make with the children of Israel in the land of Moab, besides the covenant which He made with them in Horeb.*
>
> *Deuteronomy 29:1 NKJV*

Notice the words, "besides the covenant which He made with them in Horeb." The covenant referred to in Horeb was given through Moses on Mount Sinai 40 years before.

The Palestinian Covenant is detailed in Deuteronomy 27 through 29, in which God gave Moses a specific covenant for the people who were about to enter and take the land of Canaan. In Deuteronomy 29:5, Moses says, "And I have led you forty years in the wilderness," illustrating that the Palestinian covenant presented just before Moses' death was linked with but separate from the Mosaic covenant.

The Mosaic covenant was made at Mount Sinai in Horeb. The Palestinian covenant was made in the land of Moab. The Mosaic covenant was geared toward the conduct of the people with God—they were told to love God with all their heart, mind and strength—and toward the conduct of the people in relation to one another. The Palestinian covenant focused more upon laws governing their right to abide in the land.

Especially in Deuteronomy 27 and 28, the Palestinian covenant detailed the blessings for obedience and the curses for disobedience to the Mosaic covenant. Obedience would cause them to flourish and prosper, to be in health and be free from their enemy's dominance. Disobedience would bring failure and heartache, eventually leading to captivity, slavery and expulsion from the land.

Therefore keep the words of this covenant, and do them, that you may prosper in all that you do. All of you stand today before the Lord your God: your leaders and your tribes and your elders and your officers, all the men of Israel, your little ones and your wives—also the stranger who is in your camp, from the one who cuts your wood to the one who draws your water—that you may enter into covenant with the Lord your God, and into His oath, which the Lord your God makes with you today, that He may establish you today as a people for Himself, and that He may be God to you, just as

He has spoken to you, and just as He has sworn to your fathers, to Abraham, Isaac, and Jacob. I make this covenant and this oath, not with you alone, but with him who stands here with us today before the Lord our God, as well as with him who is not here with us today... so that there may not be among you man or woman or family or tribe, whose heart turns away today from the Lord our God...

Deuteronomy 29:9-15, 18 NKJV

Because He perfectly kept the law and observed to do what was written in the book of the law, including the blessings of Deuteronomy 27-29, Jesus walked in health and He prospered in all He did. Because He came under the authority of this covenant, He came under the care of this covenant. It also meant that He could impart with authority the health, well-being, protection, and prosperous conditions promised in this covenant.

Jesus could walk throughout the land of Israel with confidence that He was fully following the conditions required of Him to live safely in the land free of dominance from His enemies, including the motivating spirit and attitude behind any natural enemies. This energized His movements and helped empower every conflict Jesus had with the devil and demon spirits. Jesus had a right to occupy territory in the land, and He had the authority to expel sickness and disease, and authority to cast out demons and evil spirits that would dare cross His path in the land.

Jesus walked in the earthly authority that each of the covenants promised. Through the Davidic covenant, Jesus would walk in the royal kingdom rights of a king in the earth.

The Davidic Covenant

God made the Davidic covenant with David following the death of Jonathan and King Saul, and after David had been officially enthroned at Jerusalem. This covenant ultimately served as a direct road to an everlasting throne and an everlasting kingdom for Jesus as the King of Kings. The Davidic covenant is a continuation, reinforcement, and elaboration of the Abrahamic covenant. The primary promise of the Davidic covenant is centered on the kingship of David and his sons, the greatest of whom is the Lord Jesus Christ.

A kingly heritage was promised in the Abrahamic covenant to Abraham and Sarah, and later to Jacob and his son, Judah.

> *I will make you exceedingly fruitful; and I will make nations of you, and kings shall come from you. And I will establish My covenant between Me and you and your descendants after you in their generations, for an everlasting covenant to be God to you and your descendants after you.*

> *Genesis 17:6-7 NKJV*

Notice here in Genesis that God established the legal precedent for every one of Abraham's descendants to be partakers of what's promised in Abraham's covenant. David's reign as king was fulfilling what God said to Abraham. This covenant promise that kings would come through Abraham's family was likewise stated to David and through his family. This covenant promise also spoke directly of and to Jesus as King and of His everlasting kingdom.

And it shall be, when your days are fulfilled, when you must go to be with your fathers, that I will set up your seed after you, who will be of your sons; and I will establish his kingdom. He shall build Me a house, and I will establish his throne forever. I will be his Father, and he shall be My son; and I will not take My mercy away from him, as I took it from him who was before you. And I will establish him in My house and in My kingdom forever; and his throne shall be established forever.

1 Chronicles 17:11-14 NKJV

With this covenant, there was an immediate promise that one of David's sons would sit on his throne. This was important because in those times, the nations around Israel often had a different transition plan from king to king. Frequently when one king died or was killed, the throne wasn't always given to a son of the king. Many times, there would be an uprising and power struggle with a new family coming into power, especially in the cases where the king was killed by enemies. When that happened, the new regime would seek out and kill all the sons and relatives of the previous king.

God was promising David that there would always be one of his sons assumimg the throne. This covenant was providing security for the safety of David's descendants. It was also speaking of an everlasting kingdom where one of David's seed would reign as king forever. This is where and how the authority of the Davidic covenant extended to Jesus.

Jesus understood that His authority included reigning as king over an everlasting kingdom, but He also understood the way in which this kingdom would be set up. The disciples of Jesus' day thought it was going to begin in the earth while Jesus was here in the land of Israel. There was even a time when the multitudes wanted to make Jesus a king. He was performing miraculous signs in healing the diseased and had just multiplied five barley loaves and two small fish to feed over five thousand people, and the people were mobilizing to crown Jesus as a king.

> *Therefore when Jesus perceived that they were about to come and take Him by force to make Him king, He departed again to the mountain by Himself alone.*
>
> *John 6:15 NKJV*

Not long after Jesus' resurrection, His followers were

expecting Jesus to assume the role of King and deliver them from Roman occupation and oppression. You can imagine their desire for it to be so. They had been under the government of Rome and felt the sting from being subject to Roman rule for many years with no apparent end in sight. They were remembering the works Jesus performed before His death, and now stood in a sense of awe and hope following His resurrection.

One of the most valuable things to learn from the life of Jesus is the restraint with which He operated in life. Just think of all the things He could have done with His authority, with His words and power, yet He was very strategic and timely in His operation of authority. When He was challenged by His own brothers to show Himself openly at the Feast of Tabernacles as the Messiah, Jesus said to them, "My time has not yet come…You go up to this feast. I am not yet going up to this feast, for My time has not yet fully come."

Not long after this discussion with His brothers, He did go secretly and discreetly to the feast, but Jesus wasn't going to be manipulated, goaded, or flattered into exerting His kingly authority outside of His timing. Not even the threat of death could force Jesus ahead of His right time to rule and reign in the earth as a sitting King. On the way to the cross, under interrogation before Pontius Pilate, He was directly asked by Pilate, "Are You the King of the Jews?"

Jesus answered, "My kingdom is not of this world. If My kingdom were of this world, My servants would fight, so that I should not be delivered to the Jews; but now My kingdom is not from here." Pilate therefore said to Him, "Are You a king then?" Jesus answered, "You say rightly that I am a king. For this cause I was born, and for this cause I have come into the world, that I should bear witness to the truth. Everyone who is of the truth hears My voice."

John 18:36-37 NKJV

Jesus' assertions that He was a king, that He had a kingdom, that He was the chief representative of truth, and that He spoke with authority to voice the truth were based on all the covenants leading up to the New Covenant, but especially the Abrahamic and Davidic covenants. Jesus was walking in the authority of Abraham and David when He confirmed His place as a king.

His place as king through the Abrahamic and Davidic covenant included dominion over His enemies. While on trial, being scourged, and crucified, it would seem that Jesus was being dominated by His enemies, but the reality was that Jesus was accomplishing every purpose that His authority through covenant made possible.

To pay the price for a man's sin, Jesus had to have the birthright authority of being a human and have the blessing and dominion given by the Edenic covenant. To redeem man, He had to operate in the authority of the Adamic covenant that only the redeemer could use. To fully restore man's purpose, He had to accept the authority of the Noahic covenant. To be legally endorsed to be the Messiah, He had to come through the seed and authority of the Abrahamic covenant.

To qualify His claims, to fulfill the payment price for sin, He had to perfectly fulfill the law in the authority of the Mosaic covenant. To legally abide in the land of His lineage in dominion over His enemies, He had to walk in the authority of the Palestinian covenant. And now, to abide as the everlasting king on an everlasting throne, and as ruler over an everlasting kingdom, Jesus had to assume the authority of the Davidic covenant.

Included in the Davidic covenant was dominion over enemies.

> *And I have been with you wherever you have gone, and have cut off all your enemies from before you, and have made you a name like the name of the great men who are on the earth...Also I will subdue all your enemies.*
>
> *I Chronicles 17:8, 10 NKJV*

Notice in Psalm 18 how David recounts his dominion over enemies.

*I have pursued my enemies and overtaken them;
neither did I turn back again till they were destroyed.
I have wounded them, so that they could not rise;
they have fallen under my feet. For you have armed
me with strength for the battle; you have subdued
under me those who rose up against me. It is God
who avenges me, and subdues the people under me;
He delivers me from my enemies. You also lift me up
above those who rise against me; you have delivered
me from the violent man.*

Psalm 18:37-39, 47-48 NKJV

David credits God with girding him with strength, subduing those that rose against him, delivering him from his enemies and from the violent man. But notice that at the same time he says that he (David) pursued his enemies and overtook them, consumed them, wounded them, and put them under his feet. Which was it? Both. When David assumed his place of authority, God's authority could flow through him in the earth. This is how it works for each one of us, too.

People many times think that if something's going to happen, God's going to do it all and they have no role or responsibility. That's not how David thought. He knew that if it wasn't for God's help and protection, he would have been utterly defeated. But he also knew that God's authority and power had to have a willing vessel through which to flow into the earth.

Where does this place of authority find its beginning expressions for David? Look at the beginning of Psalm 18 and hear the heart of a man who knew, reverenced and worshipped God as the source of his authority and victory in life.

> *I will love You, O Lord, my strength. The Lord is my rock and my fortress and my deliverer; my God, my strength, in whom I will trust; my shield and the horn of my salvation, my stronghold. I will call upon the Lord, who is worthy to be praised; so shall I be saved from my enemies.*
>
> *Psalm 18:1-3 NKJV*

David knew his place under God. He exalted in it as He recognized, honored, and praised God. This is so important to the one that will speak in the voice of authority with impact. The voice we speak with is done so with reverence and praise toward God. It's done while constantly noting how it is God who gives us strength, and it is God who is our firm foundation and the rock of stability upon which we stand.

It is God who is our impregnable fortress of protection, and it is God who delivers us from the most precarious of situations. God is the person and object of our trust and our shield of defense. It is God who is the horn of our salvation. This word horn carries with it the meaning of authority, so this means that God is the authority of our salvation, our deliverance, protection, preservation, healing, and wholeness. And it is God who is our stronghold. As we continually honor and reverence God, as we maintain Him as first place and final authority in our lives, He keeps us close to Himself and holds us within the security of His strength.

It is from this place that we call upon the Lord in the voice of authority and give praise. We commend Him for who He is, who He's made us to be, what He can do through us and what we can do through His strength in us.

Jesus knew this Psalm and the voice of authority revealed in it. Jesus lived his life in the midst of the beliefs stated in these verses. As He did with the other covenants, Jesus lived from the authority of David's covenant. And like David did, Jesus put into practice the lifestyle of praise for specific reasons. Praise expressed in the voice of authority is an authority expressed with reverence and respect for the giver and source of authority. When we speak like God, from a heart in harmony with God and with a nature that's reflecting God, our enemies are rendered silent.

When we speak with the voice of authority, we are taking dominion over the works of God's hands, and putting His and our enemies under foot.

Out of the mouth of babes and nursing infants you have ordained strength, because of your enemies, that you may silence the enemy and the avenger. You have

made him (man) to have dominion over the works of
Your hands, You have put all things under his feet...

Psalm 8:2, 6 NKJV

The voice of authority directs and imposes its will against the source of the problems faced. Going back to the story from Mark 4, Jesus spoke to the source of the storm: the enemy and the wind. The fear and the waves were the symptoms. The sinking of the boat and the death of Jesus and the disciples was the enemy's objective.

Remember, Jesus "rebuked" the wind and then spoke to the sea. From the roots of this word "rebuke," it also means "to direct and superimpose values, reverence and honor upon." Jesus directed and superimposed His reverence, value, and honor of the word of God upon and over the circumstances, and upon and over his soul. In other words, rebuke takes on the meaning of exercising authority over opposing forces. Jesus clothed Himself with the authority that was delegated to Him within all of the covenants when He rebuked the wind and sea and, by connection, the enemy.

Remember the meaning within the word for "beat" in Mark 4:37? "Beat," as it's used here refers to a person or personality. The personality operating behind all difficulties and the core opposition to the Word and knowledge of God is Satan. Whenever you feel opposition beating against the will of God, it's coming from the sole opposition that the enemy has toward all things God.

This also reinforces two important points about using the voice of authority. First, God is not our problem. God is never our problem. God is our answer and the Source of all our solutions. Always stay on God's side. Staying on the right side of God is far more important than staying on the right side of people or history.

Second, people are not our problem. People can be channels through which a problem may be presented, but the source of the problem is what's behind the behavior of people. This is why we must resist solely arguing against people, or fighting against people as if there are no underlying forces at work, or judging people as if we ourselves have never missed the mark of what's right. Paul made this clear when he wrote to the Ephesians on where to focus the release of their authority.

> *For we do not wrestle against flesh and blood, but against principalities, against powers, against the rulers of the darkness of this age, against spiritual hosts of wickedness in the heavenly places.*
>
> *Ephesians 6:12 NKJV*

We do have an enemy in the earth. There is opposition to living for God. Problems do arise, but when they arise, release the voice of authority against circumstances, conditions, the enemy, and all his maneuvers and operations in the earth, but never directly as a weapon against people as the problem. I'm not saying we can't speak authoritatively to be an effective leader of people, to communicate instructions to a group of people or even to bring correction to people as needed. If we have to do so, we speak the truth firmly, but we speak the truth in love.

I am saying we never use our authority to demean or diminish the value of a person. We don't speak with the voice of authority to intimidate or manipulate people nor do we use the voice of authority to attract inappropriate attention to our spiritual authority and dominion in the earth.

Jesus used the voice of authority by superimposing the values of God against the personal desires of the enemy. This allowed His authority to change His circumstances instead of His circumstances changing His soul and minimizing the expression of his authority. In the midst of a great storm, Jesus maintained rule over His own spirit and kept His mouth and His tongue in line with His will to release authority that worked well for Him.

He who is slow to anger is better than the mighty; and he who rules his spirit than he who takes a city.

Proverbs 16:32 NKJV

Whoever guards his mouth and tongue keeps his soul from troubles.

Proverbs 21:23 NKJV

The word for "rules" in Proverbs 16:32 means "has power over, has dominion over, is the governor of." Problems were either avoided or overcome in Jesus' life because He kept Himself under the authority of the covenants and spoke from this authority as the governor and one with power and dominion over His own spirit.

Jesus came to fulfill all the old covenant requirements, but it was done in the light of a new and better way of living, a new and better covenant to come. What Jesus did in submitting to the authority of the prior covenants was vital toward establishing the validity and benefits of the new covenant. Let's look at some of the main points of this new covenant and how they relates to your use of the voice of authority.

The New Covenant

The new covenant is called not only new but better than the old. Whenever we say something is better, we can assume that the new includes the same features and quality of what was old and has made upgrades that make what's new better than what's old. Every year, automobile companies release new models that typically introduce some new things, higher quality components, better engine function, more luxury items that hopefully present a better value for the money being spent. You don't say a new product is better than the old if the new has fewer and poorer features, less functionality, decreased quality and a diminished value in comparison with the old product.

God made the New Covenant through our covenant partner, friend and brother, the Lord Jesus Christ. "Jesus is Lord" is stating and clearly communicating His place as the supreme head over the corporate spiritual entity known as the kingdom of God. He is also the one who entered covenant with God on man's behalf. The New Covenant is the culmination of all other covenants and is the entrance point into the Everlasting Covenant.

The primary problem with all the previous covenants was that man's heart and nature was not yet changed and made right with God. Man's very nature was foreign to God's nature. With the introduction of the New Covenant, all of this changed. Let's explore what a few of the Old Testament prophets had to say about the covenant to come.

> *"Behold, the days are coming, says the Lord, when I will make a new covenant with the house of Israel and with the house of Judah—Not according to the covenant that I made with their fathers in the day that I took them by the hand to lead them out of the land of Egypt, My covenant which they broke, though I was a husband to them, says the Lord. But this is the covenant that I will make with the house of Israel after those days, says the Lord: I will put My law in their minds, and write it on their hearts; and I will be their God, and they shall be My people. No more shall every*

man teach his neighbor, and every man his brother,
saying, 'Know the Lord,' for they all shall know Me,
from the least of them to the greatest of them, says the
Lord. For I will forgive their iniquity, and their sin I
will remember no more."

Jeremiah 31:31-34 NKJV

Jeremiah received revelation of a new covenant while Israel endured times of national distress. We'll see this in more detail when we discuss Hebrews 8, but here in Jeremiah's writings we see four elements presented in Jeremiah 31 that would be present and available in the new covenant.

I will give you a new heart and put a new spirit
within you; I will take the heart of stone out of your
flesh, and give you a heart of flesh. I will put my spirit
within you, and cause you to walk in my statutes, and
you will keep my judgments, and do them.

Ezekiel 36:26-27 NKJV

Ezekiel highlights one of the greatest truths and benefits of the new covenant. The one who enters into the new covenant would be given a new heart and a new spirit. The core and nature of new covenant believers would be equipped with the core and nature of God endorsed with full authority to live from the base and root of the life of God.

And additionally, God said He would put His Spirit

within the new covenant believer. We're given the equipment, resources, consultant and coach inside of us. It would be like someone being given excessive and unlimited resources, a life changing and constantly needed product, cutting edge equipment to make that product, the best most highly skilled work force servicing that product, elite executive and management leadership and salespeople, and then being told to build a company in an inviting and favorable country. Imagine having every component for peak performance and exceptional success within your grasp. This is what the new covenant provides.

I also want you to notice a key phrase surrounding God's promise of a new heart and new spirit. God said, "I will." His will is always representative of an expected outcome that's guaranteed and backed by His authority. God authorizes every new covenant believer to experience a new heart and new spirit in full totality of experience.

The new covenant relationship God established is simple to understand at face value, yet very sophisticated and substantial as to all its components and what's available to us as new covenant believers.

Moreover I will make a covenant of peace with them; and it shall be an everlasting covenant with them: I will establish them and multiply them, and I will set My sanctuary in their midst forevermore. My tabernacle also shall be with them; indeed I will be their God, and they shall be My people.

Ezekiel 37:26-27 NKJV

Ezekiel also wrote about a covenant of peace—not only the absence of chaos, but the presence of wholeness, security, and well-being. It is one thing to know someone is supportive of you, but totally another thing for that support to be faithfully, vigorously and increasingly demonstrated. God wasn't just saying He would look caringly down upon us and wish us well. He was saying He would live in and among us. Forever. That's security. That's covenant.

I, the LORD, have called You in righteousness, and will hold Your hand, and will keep You, and give You as a covenant of the people, as a light of the Gentiles to open blind eyes, to bring out prisoners from the prison, those who sit in darkness from the prison house.

Isaiah 42:6-7 NKJV

Isaiah wrote about one of the greatest truths regarding the new covenant. Jesus is the covenant partner on behalf of man with God, and at the same time, He's the covenant partner on behalf of God with man. He's the Word made flesh. Covenants are ratified through words in blood. Jesus' blood gives life to flesh, but also gives life to the covenant. Jesus was given in flesh, in blood, and in Word as a covenant of the people. This new covenant also became a light of the world outside of Israel—the Gentile world. Light opens eyes to see, shows the way out of imprisonment, and gives a path to follow from being oppressed and beat down by generations of being enslaved to a darkened nature.

All of these Old Testament writers pointed to a covenant to come delivered in the body and life of Jesus. It was a covenant that would bring a new and better hope, not only for Israel, but for the entire world, all of the human race. It would signal the beginnings of fulfilling the word God gave to Abram, telling him that through his family all the families of the earth would be blessed. The writer of Hebrews quoted Jeremiah and Ezekiel in explaining that this new covenant would be better and more excellent than the previous covenants.

> *But now He has obtained a more excellent ministry, inasmuch as He is also Mediator of a better covenant, which was established on better promises. For if that first covenant had been faultless, then no place would have been sought for a second. Because finding fault with them, He says: "Behold, the days are coming, says the Lord, when I will make a new covenant with the house of Israel and with the house of Judah—not according to the covenant that I made with their fathers in the day when I took them by the hand to lead them out of the land of Egypt; because they did not continue in My covenant, and I disregarded them, says the Lord. For this is the covenant that I will make with the house of Israel after those days, says the Lord:*

I will put My laws in their mind and write them on their hearts; and I will be their God, and they shall be My people. None of them shall teach his neighbor, and none his brother, saying, 'Know the Lord,' for all shall know Me, from the least of them to the greatest of them. For I will be merciful to their unrighteousness, and their sins and their lawless deeds I will remember no more." In that He says, "A new covenant," He has made the first obsolete. Now what is becoming obsolete and growing old is ready to vanish away.

Hebrews 8:6-13 NKJV

This passage in Hebrews 8:6-13 highlights four key points to the New Covenant.

1. I will put my laws into their mind, and write them in their hearts.
2. I will be their God, and they shall be My people.
3. They shall all know Me, from the least to the greatest.
4. I will forgive their iniquities, and I will remember their sins no more.

The last blessing named is the root of this New Covenant: complete and total pardon of sin accompanied by the rooting out of the sin nature and the deposited installation of the new nature in Christ. This can only be accomplished by being given a new heart and a new spirit, as Ezekiel 36:26-27 explained. One of the core demands of the Old Covenant

154

was for Israel to hear and obey the voice of God through whatever form in which He spoke. God desired obedience from the heart.

Then I will give them an heart to know me, that I am the LORD; and they shall be My people, and I will be their God, for they shall return to Me with their whole heart.

Jeremiah 24:7 NKJV

True, genuine, sincere obedience could only be done from a changed nature. This empowerment to obey from the heart is what the New Covenant gives man. God Himself teaches us through the Holy Spirit to help us understand what He says in His word is our covenant right.

When a person is changed from the inside out, made to be a new creation—a new spiritual species compatible with the very nature of God Himself—that person is capable of functioning in a level of authority that exceeds the one with an unchanged nature. The problem is found in New Covenant people making the choice to operate and live at a level beneath the authority built into us as believers under the New Covenant. And in large part, it's because of a failure to recognize the primary position that words are to play in our lives.

Perhaps we've grown so accustomed to the common

place use of words for information or as a way to fill the time that the true value of words has been lost upon us. And as we've lost insight about our authority as speaking spirits, it seems we've significantly diminished the spiritual value God placed in us to be able to speak with a voice that carries substantial and life-changing authority. Words dominate our lives on a daily basis, but it's time for us to learn how to dominate and transform our lives with the words we speak each day.

Chapter 7

Words Dominate Our Lives

You may or may not have caught ahold of these next few statements before, but just in case, let me remind you of a few things. Man was created with words by God. Man was made a speaking spirit in the image and likeness of God. The earth is a planet created through and constantly affected by words. Words are ever present throughout our lives. The earth is a word planet dominated by words. Words dominate our lives.

In this word based world, Jesus was highly developed and skilled in how He used His words. He walked like a man and talked like God, and based on everything we've looked at throughout every area we've looked at, it should be pretty evident that we are authorized to do the same. But we must learn how to use our voice like Jesus used His voice, release our authority the same way Jesus did, and transform our lives the same way Jesus did for so many with His words.

How could Jesus walk and talk in this manner with such confidence? One reason is because He used angelic resources available to Him.

*Bless the Lord, you His angels, who excel in strength,
who do His word, heeding the voice of His word.*

Psalm 103:20 NKJV

Notice how the New American Bible (NAB) translates
Psalm 103:20.

*Bless the Lord, all you His angels, mighty in strength,
who do His bidding, obeying His spoken word.*

Psalm 103:20 NAB

When we speak the word of God as the will of God for
us, we authorize and release all the might and strength of
angels to fully participate in the fulfillment of our spoken
words. Unseen to the physical eye, angels are ministering
spirits sent to minister on behalf of the heirs of salvation.
Jesus acknowledged His authority to engage angels on His
behalf. When He was betrayed by Judas in the garden of
Gethsemane and facing Roman soldiers, Peter drew his
sword in defense, but Jesus said to him, "Do you think that
I cannot now pray to My Father, and He will provide Me
with more than twelve legions of angels?"

Let's think back again on our explanation of what
happened in Mark 4, and let's pick up what took place
following Jesus' demonstration of the voice of authority to
save His disciples from capsizing in the sea.

And they came over unto the other side of the sea...

Mark 5:1 KJV

Mission accomplished! It came to pass exactly the way Jesus said it would before they left. Jesus said, "Let us pass over to the other side." He spoke from His heart what He believed, and His words came to pass.

> *For verily I say unto you, That whosoever shall say unto this mountain, Be thou removed, and be thou cast into the sea; and shall not doubt in his heart, but shall believe that those things which he saith shall come to pass; he shall have whatsoever he saith.*

Mark 11:23 KJV

But there was a greater purpose than just having something come to pass for the sake of proving that the laws of faith and confession and that the voice of authority work in the storms of life you may personally face. We must understand that Jesus did nothing unless it had a purpose. In crossing over to the other side of the sea, Jesus was fulfilling an assignment from the Father. There was a demon possessed man who was terrorizing the coast on the other side of the sea, and Jesus was following ordered steps to free the coasts of darkness and terror by freeing this man from bondage and oppression.

Jesus demonstrated the living truth of faith and confession in Mark 11:23 with how He spoke to a fig tree and commanded it to shrivel and die from the roots. He also showed the effects of faith released in the voice of authority when He conquered the winds and stilled the waves on a storm driven sea in Mark 4.

But there was a greater purpose than just having something come to pass for the sake of proving that the laws of confession and the voice of authority work in the challenges and storms of life you may personally face. We must understand that Jesus did nothing unless it had a purpose. In crossing over to the other side of the sea Jesus was fulfilling an assignment from the Father. There was a demon possessed man who was terrorizing the coast on the other side of the sea and Jesus was following ordered steps to free the coasts of darkness and terror by freeing this man from bondage and oppression.

Then they came over to the other side of the sea, to the country of the Gadarenes. And when He had come out of the boat, immediately there met Him out of the tombs a man with an unclean spirit, who had his dwelling among the tombs; and no one could bind him, not even with chains, because he had often been bound with shackles and chains. And the chains had been pulled apart by him, and the shackles broken in pieces; neither could anyone tame him and always, night and day, he was in the mountains and in the tombs, crying out and cutting himself with stones.

Mark 5:1-5 NKJV

In this encounter in this region, Jesus was operating in the authority of Adam, Abraham and David. Jesus was being directed by the word God spoke in His heart about the present matter and conditions at hand and by the written word that He would have found in Isaiah on where to go and what to do. He listened to His Father's voice on the timing to act on certain instructions He knew from the written Word. Matthew 4 details Jesus' movements and shows how these movements were drawn from what Isaiah wrote and prophesied.

And leaving Nazareth, He came and dwelt in Capernaum, which is by the sea, in the borders of Zebulun and Naphtali: that it might be fulfilled which was spoken by Isaiah the prophet, saying, "The land of Zebulun, and the land of Naphtali, by the way of the sea, beyond the Jordan, Galilee of the Gentiles; the people who sat in darkness have seen a great light; and upon those who sat in the region and shadow of death Light has dawned."

Matthew 4:13-16 NKJV

The light which had sprung up was Jesus, the Light of the world. The Gadarene demoniac was a man who sat in darkness, and contributed to the people of that region sitting in darkness and under the shadow of death. Isaiah said a great Light would emerge to scatter the darkness and cause it to flee.

Nevertheless the gloom will not be upon her who is distressed, as when at first He lightly esteemed the land of Zebulun and the land of Naphtali, and afterward more heavily oppressed her, by the way of the sea, beyond the Jordan, in Galilee of the Gentiles. The people who walked in darkness have seen a great light; those who dwelt in the land of the shadow of death, upon them a light has shined.

Isaiah 9:1-2 NKJV

Mark 4 and 5 took place against the Galilee coastal area. And this man and that region was set free by the voice of authority in the earth. What was destined to happen from the foundations of the world came to pass, just like God intends for all of His word to bear fruit in the earth, never returning void to Him. Many times we read the scriptures as historical accounts of Jesus and miss the point that Jesus came to demonstrate what life in the earth was meant to be like for a man or woman anointed and authorized by God. The same inherent truths and principles by which Jesus lived are the same ones by which we are to live, see, and experience the benefits contained within these truths and principles.

Look at these two complimentary statements God made about Himself, and let's recognize and adopt the truths and

162

principles here for our own lives.

> *Declaring the end from the beginning, and from ancient times things that are not yet done, saying, My counsel shall stand, and I will do all My pleasure." Calling a bird of prey from the east, the man who executes My counsel, from a far country. Indeed I have spoken it; I will also bring it to pass. I have purposed it, I will also do it.*
>
> *Isaiah 46:10-11 NKJV*

> *I have declared the former things from the beginning; they went forth from My mouth, and I caused them to hear it. Suddenly I did them, and they came to pass. Even from the beginning I have declared it to you; before it came to pass I proclaimed it to you...*
>
> *Isaiah 48:3, 5 NKJV*

This is God's method of operation in the kingdom of God. He determines the intended outcome, declares that outcome from the outset, and stands firm in His counsel in faith. Faith is what pleases God and is involved in the expression of Him doing all His pleasure. This ancient law of confession has stood throughout eternity as the means to creating reality and building the images and experiences we desire in life.

But how does this work on a practical level? Plant your seed, speak to your mountains, and decree your desired future.

Don't spend all your time talking about your problems. Talk *to* them, and tell them the way things are going to be! Think about how you want things to be. Be specific. Think and see what life looks and feels like with the changes you need and desire already in place. Now this is the crux of the matter. If you can't see it, you can't say it in the form and fashion and with the force needed, for you to be and have it—whatever "it" is that you need and desire.

But if you can get that image settled within and be diligent and consistent to say what you want to have, things can and will be different. Decree what you need. Decree it in this present moment and hereafter with consistency. Speak your desired result on the basis of the Word of God written and the word of God spoken directly to you in your heart. You have to commit to this. It doesn't just happen because one day you voiced a positive thought or for a few days spoke a desired long term outcome. Say what you want, say what you're authorized to have, and make it a habit.

We all can appreciate the fact that God is able to do great things quickly and suddenly, yet many of the things that happen suddenly are based in a continued way of speaking and habit of doing the Word in areas of our lives. This is where so many people get discouraged or disgusted with faith and confession. They were either turned from hearing, or were insufficiently taught, that faith and confession is what we live by. The just shall live by faith. The just shall speak by faith. The just will live by what they say most consistently.

164

It's unnecessary to distract yourself with the argument of whether this is engaging in "works." Think in terms of effort. You must expend an effort mentally, emotionally, spiritually, and physically in order to maintain charge over your mouth and the words you allow out of your mouth. If this was easy and required no effort, the church would be filled with repetitively successful, one-time "word confessors." The bottom line is most people do not yet give a consistent account of words spoken in line with God's word and will for their lives, and usually don't consistently speak what they want to have in their lives. Most people are consistently *saying what they have*, saying what they don't desire, instead of consistently *saying what they want* that they do desire.

As we stand on the brink, on the very edge and precipice of the great revival and harvest of souls prepared for end times, our willing participation and declaration of this reality is a primary key to its fulfillment in the earth. Now is the time for us to press in, persevere, prepare, and train for our roles and places during this divine time in the earth. Now is when we must develop in the eternal purpose for our birth and appearance in the earth. We must assert the same degree and magnitude for understanding our specific, definite, and personal purpose for existing as we do in seeking to do our jobs or to enjoy our hobbies. You don't have to be a full time minister to do this, but now is the time to dig into the fulfillment of your potential and purpose by training and preparing in earnest.

How do these last few thoughts fit into the overall context of the topic we've been talking about? Our words take on greater force when our purpose assumes greater clarity and authority. Job 6:25 says, *"How forceful are right words!"* Choosing the right words can make a world of difference. The impact and influence of words that have the force of being right adds an undeniable elegance and effect. Speaking words in this fashion is likened to a person skilled at putting brush and paint to a blank space.

When an artist captures a picture on a canvas with perfect symmetry and proportion, with the right colors and tones, the heart of the beholder is touched as greatly as the eye. Inspiration and enlightenment can come in a way that is transformational in the life of one who sees a picture that carries a thousand forceful words. The same is true of the person who can speak a phrase of forceful words that ingrains the image of inspiration. President John F. Kennedy launched a multitude of lives into self-less service with the words, "Ask not what your country can do for you, but what you can do for your country."

Ecclesiastes 8:4 states, "Where the word of a king is, there is power..." A king sits in authority. A king sits with clarity in that authority. A king with purpose can move a nation, a region, the world to action and results. Jesus is a King—the King of kings. Each of us as believers are in position to rule as kings in life through Jesus Christ. In our own personal lives, we have a life sphere around us, a place where decisions and influence are found and used. When we understand our purpose in this sphere, we talk and act much differently than when we're wandering around confused and absent of guiding purpose. And in that wandering manner of life and confused frame of mind, we neglect to use words for their right purpose and in the authority for which they were made to be released.

What would you say if someone were to ask you, "What is the primary purpose for words?" Most people would say to transfer information or for the communication of thoughts, ideas, instructions, and emotions. If you answered this way, you wouldn't necessarily be incorrect, just incomplete.

The primary purpose for words is the creation of worlds in which to live, and correspondingly, to create environments to support living in those worlds. Jesus "authored" His environment and circumstances through the vehicle and on the basis of spoken words.

In the beginning, God created the heavens and the earth, and formed man from the dust of the earth, and breathed into him the breath of life. God created His environment and circumstances on the basis of spoken words. God established the provision that would be in the world in which He placed man. He then empowered and equipped man to use the same process of words to affect the environment in which he lived. Adam named the creatures on the earth. Ultimately, it was this power to use or not use words that relinquished authority in the earth to the enemy.

Everybody wants to be considered a winner in life. Everybody wants to come out better than they were before the start of a thing. Winning words are dominating words. Dominating words help us come out better than we were before. Winning words are rooted in the dominion that God released into our lives through the victory of Jesus overcoming the world. Authority is delegated power and influence. Dominion means to have supreme ruling authority, power, and mastery. Authority is released through words. God used His words to express and establish His dominion in and over all things. The key to authority and dominion, or mastery, is found in your words. To exercise authority and dominion, master your words.

Paul tapped into the significance and necessity of prayer in connection with words that dominate. He emphasized the need for utterance and boldness—accurate use of language and authority in the expression of that language. Prayer is the means by which we can make specific requests and receive specific directions on what to say in all the affairs of life.

In focused prayer, we can release commands that set up and direct our way. Prayer, particularly praying in the Spirit, will show us how to articulate answers to problems, speak out solutions to adversities, and reveal how to specifically define and declare with precision the things and conditions you desire in life.

And (pray) for me, that utterance may be given unto me, that I may open my mouth boldly to make known the mystery of the gospel, For which I am an ambassador in bonds: that therein I may speak boldly, as I ought to speak.

Ephesians 6:19-20 KJV

The Living Translation puts Ephesians 6:19 this way: "Pray for me, too, and ask God to give me the right words as I boldly tell others about the Lord and as I explain to them that his salvation is for the Gentiles too." Paul understood the necessity of the right words in prayer. It's important to note that you don't need a million word vocabulary to speak words that are right for you. It's a matter of searching and knowing your heart to hear the right words for you to speak in a given moment. And once you know what to speak, you must decree and declare it with boldness and confidence.

It's at that very moment that spiritual principles and godly components are set into motion. Your words of dominion initiate the movement of the kingdom machinery and divinely organized resources on your behalf. The Holy Spirit is authorized to motivate and inspire the elements of the spiritual realm to bring to pass the fullness of the words you have released. Be like God, and declare the end—the desired goal and outcome—from the beginning. Angels take to flight at the speed of light to enforce the authority and dominion uttered from your heart and through your words.

Just as God said, "Let there be light!" to change the natural conditions in the earth, you too can change the natural elements of the world around you with the words of dominion you speak with consistency. Then as Job 22:28 says, *"You shall also decree a thing, and it shall be established to you, and the light shall shine upon your ways."* The truth and principle in this verse of scripture is meant to be a primary and even daily reality in your life just like a king. Kings, or ones with a supreme level of authority, make decrees or declarations that must be obeyed. Let's look a little deeper at how this works.

Chapter 8

Dominating Words in Action

As we consider the life of King David, it's evident that he lived a life close to the heart of God. But what are the things that demonstrated this heart? It's obvious he had a heart to worship the Father. There's no doubt that he was a man of conviction, passion, and covenant. It's clear that he was able to quickly acknowledge his own wrongs and repent. He was a man committed to doing the will of God from his heart. But there's another thing that distinguished the way David lived his life. He learned the power of speaking right words to dominate his circumstances. Let's trace the path David followed that made his words powerful and dominant.

> *Now it came to pass, as David sat in his house, that David said to Nathan the prophet, Lo, I dwell in an house of cedars, but the ark of the covenant of the LORD remaineth under curtains. Then Nathan said unto David, Do all that is in thine heart; for God is with thee.*
>
> *1 Chronicles 17:1-2 KJV*

David learned throughout the course of his life that God would be with him when he followed what God put into his heart. There's a reason why David was bold as a lion when he faced Goliath. It was because he had first vanquished the lion and bear he faced in the field. Why would he even think he was prepared to fight off and overcome the ferocity of a lion and a bear? For the same reason voiced when David faced Goliath.

David was fully aware that he had the full covenant provision and protection promised as a son of Israel. David understood from what he was taught from the Torah, first books of what we have as the Bible, that the God of all creation favored Israel because Abraham believed and obeyed God. When David called Goliath an "uncircumcised Philistine" he wasn't just hurling an insult. He was stating what he had in his heart about the covenant God had made with Israel through Abraham and Moses. By believing and standing on what he had in his heart from God, David knew that God was with him.

But it happened that night that the word of God came to Nathan, saying, "Go and tell My servant David, 'Thus says the Lord: "You shall not build Me a house to dwell in. For I have not dwelt in a house since the time that I brought up Israel, even to this day, but have gone from tent to tent, and from one tabernacle to another. Wherever I have moved about with all Israel, have I ever spoken a word to any of the judges of Israel, whom I commanded to shepherd My people, saying, 'Why have you not built Me a house of cedar—'"" Now therefore, thus shall you say to My servant David, 'Thus says the Lord of hosts: "I took you from the sheepfold, from following the sheep, to be ruler over My people Israel. And I have been with you wherever you have gone, and have cut off all your enemies from before you, and have made you a name like the name of the great men who are on the earth. Moreover I will appoint a place for My people Israel, and will plant them, that they may dwell in a place of their own and move no more; nor shall the sons of wickedness oppress them anymore, as previously, since the time that I commanded judges to be over My people Israel.

1 Chronicles 17:3-10a NKJV

Through the prophet Nathan, God gave David instructions about the Temple that David had in his heart to build. Nathan encouraged David to do all that was in his heart, but God redirected David's desires. God also recounted all that He had done for David, reminding him of His faithfulness to protect and care for David and the nation of Israel.

Imagine this scene: God was speaking through the prophet to preach a personal, custom tailored message for David. David's listening to the Word, but he was also listening with the ear of the learned. He was not just hearing the words of a man but hearing the Word of God. We have it today as a passage of scripture from which we can still benefit. David had this being given to him as a word spoken by God to his heart relevant to the moment. David is hearing a reminder of past triumphs and accomplishments, but through Nathan, God also began to give insight as to the future.

> *"Also I will subdue all your enemies. Furthermore I tell you that the Lord will build you a house. And it shall be, when your days are fulfilled, when you must go to be with your fathers, that I will set up your seed after you, who will be of your sons; and I will establish his kingdom. He shall build Me a house, and I will establish his throne forever. I will be his Father, and he shall be My son; and I will not take My mercy away from him, as I took it from him who was before you. And I will establish him in My house and in My kingdom forever; and his throne shall be established forever.""" According to all these words and according to all this vision, so Nathan spoke to David.*
>
> *I Chronicles 17:10b-15 NKJV*

David has heard God speak to him in this kind of authoritative, assertive, declarative language before. In essence, God was prophesying to David through Nathan. God was defining what the future could be for David and his family. Prophecy carries great potential of a possible future made probable and tangible when people carry out the instructions and requirements to bring it to pass. Yes, God is the one who ultimately determines outcomes, but there's a definitive role the individual plays in seeing things materialize before their eyes and into their very lives.

Many times, people either remain idle awaiting God's sovereign rule to bring a prophetic declaration to pass, or they launch into immediate action without receiving further instruction and understanding. Notice what David did first with the authoritative declarations of God, because the action he takes prior to leaving the moment is crucially important.

> *Then King David went in and sat before the Lord; and he said: "Who am I, O Lord God? And what is my house, that You have brought me this far? And yet this was a small thing in Your sight, O God; and You have also spoken of Your servant's house for a great while to come, and have regarded me according to the rank of a man of high degree, O Lord God. What more can David say to You for the honor of Your servant? For You know Your servant. O Lord, for Your servant's sake, and according to Your own heart, You have done all this greatness, in making known all these great things. O Lord, there is none like You, nor is there any God besides You, according to all that we have heard with our ears. And who is like Your people Israel, the one nation on the earth whom God went to redeem for Himself as a people—to make for Yourself a name by great and awesome deeds, by driving out nations from*

before Your people whom You redeemed from Egypt?
For You have made Your people Israel Your very own
people forever; and You, Lord, have become their God.

I Chronicles 17:16-22 NKJV

"David sat in his house doing what?" Meditating on God and His word, considering ways to honor God and show his appreciation for God. Notice how David recounts God's graciousness to recognize him, and considers the favor God has bestowed upon him. As he "sat" before the Lord and thought about God's goodness and kindness, look at how David humbled himself and put God in the exalted place He deserved. He took note that God was proactive in blessing, and just like his Heavenly Father, David used his words as an initiator, self-starter, and creator.

In this exchange between God and David, God has revealed the Davidic Covenant. Covenant is delegation of authority in action, authorizing covenant partners to partake in the benefits of covenant. David came and sat before the Lord. This was a time of reflection and meditation upon, as well as the acceptance of God's promises. As he sat before the Lord, David was internalizing the vision and image God presented to him.

Notice again that David rehearsed in God's ears His greatness, and reminded Him of some of the things that He had already promised, said, and done. This wasn't done to flatter God, or to butter God up. This was done as acknowledgement of God's mercy, favor, and faithfulness, and yes, of how great and mighty God was to David. But this was also done to set spiritual principles and machinery into operation.

This is the element of true confession, or saying the same things as what God has already spoken. This wasn't a one-time activity that David stumbled upon. This was something David employed as a practice to follow as a life routine. Before speaking in the voice of authority in the earth, David sat before the Lord in consideration of the things he heard. David learned to let things spoken to him to deeply settle into his heart. He learned to let words resonate in his heart so that he could align his heart with the heart of the one who had spoken to him. And the result?

My heart was hot within me; while I was musing, the fire burned, then I spoke with my tongue:

Psalm 39:3 NKJV

David's musing was building a spiritual energy within, a momentum, so that before speaking with his tongue, he would align his heart until it burned with force so that his spoken words would dominate in life and in the world around him. His musing was a "sustained consideration" about what God had spoken to him. The longer he sustained his thoughts upon God's words, the stronger the dynamic of belief was stirred within him. And before he began to speak, he let his beliefs be bolstered by what he sustained his consideration upon.

In 2 Corinthians 4:13, Paul described what was happening in David like this: *"And since we have the same spirit of faith, according to what is written, I believed and therefore I spoke, we also believe and therefore speak..."* But Paul was quoting what David had written in Psalm 116:10 as David considered a time of distress. David was saying he would still believe in God and trust Him, and speak of his strong belief in God even when troubles surrounded him.

In 1 Chronicles 17, David isn't considering troubles but rather the blessings of God. David said to God, "You have spoken" and "You have made known all these great things." Blessing David was God's idea first. The blessing that came to all humanity in Genesis 1, and the blessing that came to rest upon Abraham in Genesis 12, and the blessings of all spiritual blessings in heavenly places in Christ (Ephesians 1:3) were all God's idea. Notice here how David speaks in connection to knowledge already revealed from the mouth of God.

"And now, O Lord, the word which You have spoken concerning Your servant and concerning his house, let it be established forever, and do as You have said. So let it be established, that Your name may be magnified forever, saying, 'The Lord of hosts, the God of Israel, is Israel's God.' And let the house of Your servant David be established before You. For You, O my God, have

revealed to Your servant that You will build him a house. Therefore Your servant has found it in his heart to pray before You.

1 Chronicles 17:23-25 NKJV

First Chronicles 17:23 in The Living Bible says, "And now I accept your promise, Lord, that I and my children will always rule this nation." David found courage, confidence, and freedom in his heart to pray and expect exactly what God promised. Knowing, acting upon and living in the revealed will of God is the place of dominion and authority.

For You, O LORD of hosts, God of Israel, have revealed this to Your servant, saying, "I will build you a house." Therefore Your servant has found it in his heart to pray this prayer to You.

2 Samuel 7:27 NKJV

This specific prayer resulted from the specific promise given to David by God. God showed David His word and His will. David was operating in the spirit of wisdom and revelation similar to the prayer Paul prayed that's found in Ephesians 1:16-23. This is how David could say, "Therefore I found in my heart what to pray." It's much like how the Spirit of truth shows us things to come.

However when He, the Spirit of truth, has come, He will guide you into all truth; for He will not speak on

His own authority, but whatever He hears He will speak; and He will tell you things to come.

John 16:13 NKJV

He shows us things for a specific purpose: to speak those things He shows you.

However, we speak wisdom among those who are mature, yet not the wisdom of this age, nor of the rulers of this age, who are coming to nothing. But we speak the wisdom of God in a mystery, the hidden wisdom which God ordained (set in place and authorized) before the ages for our glory.

I Corinthians 2:6-7 NKJV

First Corinthians 2:12-13 goes on to say that we have received the Spirit of God to know the things freely given to us, and we are to speak about these things in language given by the Holy Spirit. We need language lessons from the Holy Spirit, especially to address the natural problems, storms, and adversities in life. Of a necessity, those language lessons include speaking words that are making people and the atmosphere around us better than how we found it. Many people use their words to tear down, but we're held responsible for building people up.

Let no corrupt word proceed out of your mouth, but what is good for necessary edification, that it may impart grace to the hearers.

Ephesians 4:29 NKJV

And this right use of words isn't only to be targeted toward those around us, but we are to reject self-corrupting communications too. Our words aren't meant for tearing ourselves down by speaking negatively about ourselves. Some people speak in their own thoughts about how bad things are or will be. The thoughts we speak within are not designed to destroy our self-confidence or self-esteem, nor speak judgmentally within about other people. We are to use our words—verbalized or internalized—to build up, edify, and strengthen others and ourselves. We are to be wordsmiths that are trained and skilled in communicating from what God has placed within our hearts.

God is expecting believers to wield words to release authority, righteous authority in the earth. God is looking for us to use our gift of language well, to hone our skills, to develop in this craft to communicate to our circumstances, environment and future. Use the building blocks of words to construct a new and better future, a new and better you.

There's a reason why Jesus was so effective with His words. He knew that having God's will and word was important. Knowing God's will and word is the proper, best, and ultimate starting point, but it isn't all there is to speaking with authority. Just as David learned and Jesus displayed, we must continue by getting the will and word of God burning in the heart. We must get the will and word of God aligned in the heart. This is a vital key to speaking with an authority that is more and more effective.

In Mark 11, we have the story of Jesus speaking to a fig tree and it being cursed from the root. Mark 11:23 is Jesus teaching how and why his words worked the way they did. In parenthesis, I've included the corresponding Greek words for the English words "say" and "saith."

> *For verily I say (lego) unto you, That whosoever shall say (epo) unto this mountain, Be thou removed, and be thou cast into the sea; and shall not doubt in his heart, but shall believe that those things which he saith (lego) shall come to pass; he shall have whatsoever he saith (lego).*
>
> *Mark 11:23 KJV*

Pay close attention to the words say and saith. Both appear twice in this one verse. There are two different Greek words used here: The first word is 'lego," as in lego blocks, and the second word is "epo." I want to bring out a few more statements by Greek language scholar, Rick Renner, that will help shed additional light on these words. The word, lego, means "to lay forth (in words), to relate in words, usually of systematic or set discourse, to utter. The tense depicts a strong, stern, serious, deeply felt kind of speaking. This is not referring to a person who mutters thoughtless nonsense; this is a person who has made an inward resolution and now speaks authoritatively and with great conviction." (*Sparkling Gems From The Greek*, Rick Renner)

The word, epo, means "to speak or say (by word or writing.)" Generally, it refers to "an individual expression or speech respectively." It also means "to command, speak out and speak on."

So if we were to use these definitions and stretch this out for a fuller investigation, Mark 11:23 could be stated this way:

For truly, I consistently set forth as a systematic, set discourse and pattern, and with all resolve and authority to build this truth into you, that whosoever shall specifically and personally command this mountain, "Be removed, and be cast into the sea;" and shall not doubt in his heart, but shall believe that those things which he consistently and systematically sets forth as a vocabularic lifestyle to build truth so that it shall come to pass; he shall have whatsoever he consistently and systematically sets forth as a vocabularic lifestyle.

It's not just the one time release of authority with the hopes that it will work, it's the lifestyle of coordinating words that consistently agree with what God has said and what you believe about His will, His promises and His word, within your own heart. If Jesus had said to "speak to the mountain to be removed and cast into the sea and not doubt in your heart but believe that those things which you say in church, or once in a while, or when you're around other believers shall come to pass," Christians would have it made. But you've got to control your words outside the church and on a regular basis, no matter the setting.

Think about the woman with the issue of blood. Her story is found in Mark 5:25-34. Verse 27 says that when she had heard of Jesus, she came in the press behind, and touched his garment. Verse 28 goes on to say, "For she said..." What she heard impacted what she said. What she said impacted what she had.

In Matthew's description, Matthew 9:20-22 sheds more light on the process of saying. This passage says that she *said* "within herself." All of us have running conversations within us that define and/or describes much of what's happening outside of us. It's known as self-talk. And over time, self-talk lays an imprint on our consciousness from the inside out. Many people have these running conversations of fear, doubt and worry, but usually aren't aware that they spend hours a day deliberating on the wrong thing. The good news is they can turn it around.

You must understand that there's a great fight over your mouth and the speaking part of your faith because the authority you have as a believer must be released through words. And there's a great fight over the use of your words because speech centers in the brain exercise dominion over the whole central nervous system. If a person says, "I'm weak," or "I'm strong," the speech center in the brain sends a message out to the whole central nervous system to prepare to be either weak or strong.

Let's look at James 3 to see how it instructs on the manner and impact of the tongue and the words that come out of our mouths.

> *For we all stumble in many things. If anyone does not stumble in word, he is a perfect man, able also to bridle the whole body. Indeed, we put bits in horses' mouths that they may obey us, and we turn their whole body. Look also at ships: although they are so large and are driven by fierce winds, they are turned by a very small rudder wherever the pilot desires.*
>
> *James 3:2-4 NKJV*

The words we speak are able to control the entire experience of our bodies. Just as the bit in a horse's mouth and the rudder on a ship, the tongue turns the body in the direction determined by its owner. A horse can be turned fairly quickly in a small space, but a ship can take time and greater space to turn and change directions. The bit in the horse's mouth is likened to the will of man, and the rudder of the ship is likened to the circumstances of life a man faces.

We can change our wills quickly if we so desire, but it can take time for circumstances to line up with our change of will.

The steering wheel is in the hands of the pilot, or "governor" as the King James Version of the Bible puts it. This word "governor" means "to make straight, level and plain." This word also means "to lead or guide straight, to keep straight or direct." By choice, we have the innate capacity to make our path straight before us, and to get directly to the right places by the words we choose to come from our mouths.

It can be puzzling why anyone would purposely speak out of their mouths and over their lives oldness, weakness, confusion, an expectation of illness or worrisome outcomes, sickness, lack or any other undesirable thing. I've heard the statements that people are just trying to "keep it real" and back that up with comments that "this is just where most people live," *or* "it is what it is." The point of the matter is that when we align our hearts and words with God's will and word, we are authorized and empowered to make things be what they are meant to be in the earth, not just accept things that are not meant to be.

I'm not into lying about things or being in denial about the facts of life we face. My point is this: If according to Jesus in Mark 11:23, we can have what we say, why do people keep saying what they have and expect things to change for the better in their lives? It's within our power to initiate a change of life by what we consistently say from day to day.

Proverbs 18:21 says, "Death and life are in the power of the tongue: and they that love it shall eat the fruit thereof." This is another way of stating what we find in Mark 11:23. One of the best things about Mark 11:23 is: It will work for whosoever and it will work on whatsoever. So when the Bible says, "Let the weak say I am strong," it's a message of hope for whosoever will that needs strength for any occasion of life.

We see this mode of operation in the life of David, so let's pick up David's story again from 1 Chronicles 17 and review some key elements of what he said with the power of his tongue. In 1 Chronicles 17:23, he said to the Lord, "Let the thing You've spoken be established forever." In the same verse he said in response to what the Lord had promised to him, "Do as You have said." In verse 24, David followed it up by saying to the Lord, "Let it even be established, and "Let the house of David be established before You." He continues in verse 25 by saying, "You, Lord, told me, so therefore I found in heart to pray this before You."

God gave David what to pray and what to say. David found in his heart what to pray and what to say because he sat before the Lord to get it before he started praying and saying. Look to your heart, and you'll find where to start no matter the things that you face. Make a commitment to live in the realm of acquiring knowledge revealed by God,

then meditate it into your heart with sustained consideration. Then speak what you believe from your heart with the voice of authority.

Each of these statements we see in 1 Chronicles 17 are those of someone who has an intimate relationship with the Lord, and someone who understands the necessity of being an active participant in the relationship. These are also the words of someone who has learned that he can release authority in his life to invite God to do in the earth what God Himself has promised to do. And David discovered both what to say and what to pray by searching his heart to know what God meant in what He was saying. We are to do the same thing.

Let's consider the prayer side of things one more time. We know from Paul's writings that we are to let our requests be made known to God. John said, "This is the confidence we have in Him, that if we ask anything according to His will, He hears us. And if we know that He hears us, we know we have the petitions we desire of Him." When we do as David did and sit before the Lord to hear His heart and voice, we will make the right requests in line with His will. This is one way to be in the Spirit as we pray.

Praying always with all prayer and supplication in the Spirit, being watchful to this end with all perseverance and supplication for all saints...

Ephesians 6:18 NKJV

Let's remember for a moment that when you pray, you have to have something to say in order to pray. There is such a thing as getting into the spirit of prayer where it seems like a mantle drapes over you and you have a great sense of utterance in prayer. There is also praying in the Spirit, which is a reference to praying in other tongues.

There is also praying while being led by the Spirit. This is where you sense the direction of the Holy Spirit in prayer, and He gives you words that flow in a rhythmic fashion of speaking. It's that place of articulation, where you speak words that you see and sense in your heart. This also includes when we pray in other tongues, then listen in our hearts for interpretation as we're praying, and then release the understanding of our prayers in our known language. In this type of prayer we may pray in the spirit, then to our known language, and go back and forth, all the while expecting an understood interpretation of what we're praying.

There are times where this same being led by the Spirit can happen without praying in tongues as we yield our hearts to God and listen with sensitivity to what He wants spoken and birthed in the earth. I've had times where God would prompt me to say a phrase repeatedly regarding my health and well-being, my finances and provision, my relationships and ministry. I knew God was inspiring me to speak presently relevant and specific phrases over and over again. As I did so I could sense the inspiration of God in the words. I was aware that God had authorized me to

189

speak words to my benefit. The more I spoke the words He gave me, the more I had a sense of confidence, boldness and spiritual momentum. I felt His authority infused within my words, and in unison, I felt my authority taking effect in my circumstances.

And now, LORD, You are God, and have promised this goodness to Your servant. Now You have been pleased to bless the house of Your servant, that it may continue before You forever; for You have blessed it, O Lord, and it shall be blessed forever."

1 Chronicles 17:26-27 NKJV

When we speak specifically prompted words from the heart, it releases our authority for the thing God has spoken to us to be permitted and demonstrated in the earth on our behalf. In 1 Chronicles 17:26-27, David said, "Lord, You are God, and You have promised this goodness to me. Let it please you to bless my house forever for you bless and it is blessed forever." The same story we find in 1 Chronicles 17 is also detailed in 2 Samuel 7. Notice again how David invokes the blessing by saying the same things God has said to Him. In that moment, David was agreeing with God, saying what He said and authorizing the blessing to be demonstrated and experienced.

"Now therefore, let it please You to bless the house of Your servant, that it may continue before You forever;

for You, O Lord God, have spoken it, and with Your blessing let the house of Your servant be blessed forever."

2 Samuel 7:29 NKJV

It's very important to catch the substance in these statements David made—don't let the language be diminished and don't let the practical action David took slip by without seizing the necessity of it. Don't casually dismiss the reality of what the blessing literally means, and what it personally meant to David, his family and the nation. An amplified meaning of what encompasses being blessed is to be empowered to prosper, advance, excel, increase and have the mastery and dominion in and over all of your circumstances in spirit, soul, body, family, financially, socially, vocationally, and ministerially, in all of your thoughts, words, actions, decisions, desires, determinations, and destinies.

Being blessed by God was and is an ultimate level of experience in life, not a courtesy comment or plastic ritual. This definition undoubtedly outstrips the typical experience of believers. Yet the reality of it is available. Most people assume that the blessing is this aura that suddenly comes upon and overtakes a person somehow, and a person is either blessed or not blessed. We all know that a suddenly blessed experience marks a person's life and memory in a very notable and evident manner. But the blessing isn't meant to be occasional events that stand out from the routines of life.

191

The blessing is meant to be like a garment continually worn on a daily basis as a lifestyle. The blessing is sometimes spectacular but always supernatural. What I mean by that is that we should see the evidences of being blessed in things small, large, and everything in between. The atmosphere in our homes should be blessed. How we speak in our homes to our spouse, children, parents and siblings should contain degrees of the definition for blessed shared above.

Gratitude in the heart is revealed in words of appreciation. We live in an atmosphere of blessing every time we express our gratitude and appreciation with the people we see every day in our homes. The more gratitude we express, the more greatly we're blessed. Expressing gratitude is a way to alleviate stress and strife. You'll have a better life if you eliminate strife.

It's easy to default into expecting the people we live with to do things for us in general, or especially to do things for us that we don't particularly enjoy or want to do ourselves. The problem is that we begin to descend into a place of feeling entitled. It can become too easy to place a direct or indirect demand on people to serve us, instead of appreciating each thing done for us or our household with a word of, "Thank you. I appreciate you washing dishes, taking out the garbage, cleaning the bathroom, vacuuming the living room" or whatever it is that someone has done either directly for you or indirectly for the household.

It's a blessing to be properly and regularly appreciated. Just a quick and simple "thank you, I appreciate you doing that," performs wonders in transforming a home and household. When appreciation becomes a habit, a culture of gratitude is cultivated and created. The home becomes a place of blessing where appreciation is given and received.

Remember what Paul said about remembering the words of the Lord Jesus in Acts 20:35? "And remember the words of the Lord Jesus, that He said, 'It is more blessed to give than to receive.'" It's important to note that the Lord Jesus didn't say it's "only blessed" to give. But He did very clearly say it's "more blessed" to give. Receiving appreciation is still quite the blessing. But in the giving of appreciation between family members, a well-defined atmosphere of blessing begins to take on even greater form. By giving appreciation a much deserved place of sustained expression, the culture of appreciation establishes blessing as the ingrained feature, function and fulfillment of the household. And who doesn't want that?

The bottom line is that the blessing is a tangibly imparted authorization to live life on a greater level. It causes the recipient of blessing, and the participator in blessing to function on a higher plane with greater results. The blessing is something that can flow through a person's life to make a family, church, workplace, community, or government be the fullest expression and demonstration of the potential they possess.

When David assertively declared in 1 Chronicles 17:23-24 to let what God said to be established in his life and his family's lives, he wasn't being braggadocios or prideful, nor was he assuming a place not given to him. Look again at what he said: "Therefore now, LORD, let the thing that You have spoken concerning your servant and concerning his house be established forever, and do as You have said. Let it even be established, that Your name may be magnified forever, saying, The LORD of hosts is the God of Israel, even a God to Israel: and let the house of David Your servant be established before You."

What does this phrase, "let it be established" mean and signal? It means that I agree with what was said, so do it, make it happen, let it come to pass! I'm saying, "Let there be a demonstration and experience of what God has spoken of me!" That which God has blessed cannot be cursed. Just as God said, "Let there be, let there be, let there be" in the beginning, we have a similar right to speak to God in agreement with God, and affirm with Him that we give our authorization to let the things He's spoken of us be established. That can sound strange, but keep it in the context of agreeing with what God has already spoken to us personally, what He has made known and clear. Keep it in the context that it must match scriptures or guidelines and principles we can clearly see in scripture.

What David did in saying, "Let it be established," literally authorized and permitted God to flow every one of these pronounced blessings into his life, and into the life and development of his entire family. David purposely targeted his response to be in complete agreement with the fullness of blessing and life God had spoken and promised to him. And as a result, following this encounter with God, David became even more successful, more prosperous and blessed.

> *After this it came to pass that David attacked the Philistines, subdued them, and took Gath and its towns from the hand of the Philistines. Then he defeated Moab, and the Moabites became David's servants, and brought tribute. And David defeated Hadadezer king of Zobah as far as Hamath, as he went to establish his power by the River Euphrates. David took from him one thousand chariots, seven thousand horsemen, and twenty thousand foot soldiers. Also David hamstrung all the chariot horses, except that he spared enough of them for one hundred chariots. When the Syrians of Damascus came to help Hadadezer king of Zobah, David killed twenty-two thousand of the Syrians. Then David put garrisons in Syria of Damascus; and the Syrians became David's servants, and brought tribute. So the Lord preserved David wherever he went.*
>
> *1 Chronicles 18:1-6 NKJV*

Everywhere David went, and in everything he did, the Lord preserved him. The word for "preserved" means "to be delivered, to be liberated, to be saved in battle, to save from moral troubles and to give victory to." Everywhere David went, the Lord delivered him from his enemies, the Lord liberated and saved him in battles against physical opposition and moral troubles, and the Lord gave him victory.

But notice the beginning of this account in 1 Chronicles 18 starts with, "After this." After what? After God presented a covenant proposition to David and David accepted the proposition with a verbally declared acceptance of the terms. It's also important to remember that David had to do his part in walking the terms out in how he lived. He planned and acted strategically, and inquired of the Lord every step of the way. He used, not a one-time confession, but a pattern of declaring faith in God's covenant and then acted like one with authority to live to the full extent of the promised blessings. David was a man after God's own heart, not just because of what he believed and lived from within but also because he was a man of action who put his words into action. He made his words work for him, not against him. This is what we, too, must do.

Chapter 9

Putting Your Words To Work For You

W'll close out this book with a practical application of the voice of authority, but first we'll explore an example drawn from the book of Job. Job's life is an example of the journey of one man from a place of fear, self-justification, anger, and agitation to that of faith in the almighty God, far greater than he possessed prior to God's correction of his perspective. Job comes to the realization that God is good and God is right even when he doesn't understand everything. We too would do well to always stay on God's side. God is good. He's merciful. His truth endures to all generations, and He never changes.

Although everything in the book of Job is truly stated, everything in the book of Job isn't a statement of enduring and divine truth. In other words, the events and statements are recorded accurately, but some of the statements aren't things upon which to base your life and worldview. Job initially sought to justify himself and question God's methods. He learned that he was unqualified to judge and instruct God. It's important that we remember that Job walked in all the light and understanding he had at the time. He didn't have the New Covenant, the blood of Jesus, the word of God in scripture form, the indwelling of the Holy Spirit, the full rights of an accomplished redemption, nor the full depth of revelation to which we have access. Once Job was given an audience with God, he quickly repented and corrected his ways.

The thing to remember about Job is that Job presents a question, but Jesus is the answer. Like Job, we can come to crossroads in life and be confused about what to do when we don't know why something undesired or bad is happening to us or someone we know. I want to reiterate, "always stay on God's side." God is not our problem. He is the definitive solution and ultimate answer to any problem we could ever encounter. We can learn from Job, but we're not to be disciples of Job. We're disciples of Jesus. We're not commissioned to follow Job's example except in the ways that it conforms to the example of Jesus and godly principles drawn from scripture. Jesus is the standard and ultimate example of our reality. Jesus is exact doctrine and perfect theology.

We also are to remember that all scripture is inspired by God and is profitable for doctrine, correction, reproof, and instruction in righteousness. We are built up, edified and strengthened by the Word of God, by the word of faith and the word of His grace. Sometimes we learn what not to say and do from the examples given in the scriptures. That too is profitable and inspired by God.

With that said, there is a passage from Job 22 that genuinely reflects the heart of God for man in the earth. And I believe that from all else that's been written prior to this in the pages of Putting Your Words to Work, you can see a continuity of thought and congruence of philosophy in what we find here in Job, and in what we can see from other scriptures in both the Old Testament and the New Testament.

> *Now acquaint yourself with Him, and be at peace; thereby good will come to you. Receive, please, instruction from his mouth, and lay up His words in your heart. You will make your prayer unto Him, He will hear you, and you will pay your vows. You will also declare (decree) a thing, and it will be established for you; so light will shine on your ways.*
>
> *Job 22:21-22, 27-28 NKJV*

In the context of Job 22, we have it stated that the path to prosperity in natural things is always paved with prosperity in spiritual things, primarily and most notably rooted in a living relationship with our Heavenly Father (noted in Job 22:24-25 with the mention of the Almighty being our gold and silver). Out of that relationship and through prayer, we find the promise that we shall decree a thing and it shall be established. We are to make it our regular habit to declare and decree the things we need established in our lives.

We need to pay attention to what we say on a regular basis. I heard Kenneth E. Hagin say in a message titled, Your Words: "The words that you speak locate you. The words that you speak fixes the landmarks of your life. Or let's put it another way. Maybe you can understand it a little better. You never realize in life beyond the words that you speak." "Landmarks" are established markings and boundaries. What Brother Hagin was saying with this statement is in agreement with Job 22:28, "You will also declare (decree) a thing, and it will be established for you."

A very crucial point for you to maintain is to get the words deep down in your heart, and once you get words down in your heart and begin to proclaim them, they'll begin to rise to the surface. What you declare and decree will take form and take shape and materialize in such a way that you can see, feel, and experience what you've been saying from your heart. Refuse to limit God or limit what you're saying with a clock or calendar. A main key is lodged within continuing to consistently speak what you believe from your heart through each time of the year and season of life.

The proof of what's outlined here only comes in the continuity of doing what's required. At the beginning of this book, I wrote, "If you want something that works for a lifetime, you will find proven things that work in these pages, but it may take some time and effort to experience the

200

fullest results. Yet rest assured that once truth is settled in place, once it's in your heart, it will produce a steady stream of right results."

With that in mind, and whenever teaching or instruction comes, it's important to put learning to work as quickly as possible. You may have already started the process and are seeing some results, but as an assistance, I want to share with you a few passages of scripture that I've declared, decreed, and spoken through the years and found to be vital to my own growth, maturity, and success. I've also learned that it's important to build a habit with simplicity.

Here are three passages of scripture that you can use on a daily basis to declare and decree to help jumpstart your day in the voice of authority. The three passages are Psalm 1:1-3, I Corinthians 13:4-8a in the Amplified Bible and Psalm 91. All three are stated in a declarative and affirmational tone as a personal declaration and decree. Speaking out one after the other, this will take you approximately five minutes or less.

When you speak this way, you're imparting the Word into your day and life. You're covering your day with spiritual substance through the force of faith. You're releasing your authority to enforce the type of atmosphere and conditions you desire in your home, marriage, family, friendships, relationships, work, ministry and life. You're directing your future to new and better destinations. You're saturating your thoughts with enduring truth. You're providing the fuel to empower you on your journey day by day. You're storing up and tapping into the supply of the Word and Spirit available to you.

Remember that your words carry influence and God responds to your words that are in unity with Him and His word. In Daniel 10:10-12, an angel was dispatched on the basis of Daniel's words.

> *Suddenly, a hand touched me, which made me tremble on my knees and on the palms of my hands. And he said to me, "O Daniel, man greatly beloved, understand the words that I speak to you, and stand upright, for I have now been sent to you." While he was speaking this word to me, I stood trembling. Then he said to me, "Do not fear, Daniel, for from the first day that you set your heart to understand, and humble yourself before your God, your words were heard; and I have come because of your words.*
>
> *Daniel 10:10-12 NKJV*

When you speak from a position of respect toward God and humility under His care, God hears your words. Supernatural assistance and godly authority will come with these words. As you use these three scripture passages as a part of your foundational base, you'll also find that God expands your understanding and prompts you by His Spirit to speak other things that are personally and immediately relevant to your life.

Listen closely with the ear of the learned and you'll be given a word to speak in season, both to yourself and to those that are weary and weakened. Your words will bring measures of strength to you and to those around you. Things will change for you. Things will be better. All because of the inspired words you continually speak from the depths of your heart.

To serve as a cue for you to be consistent with this, I suggest that you either copy these declarations in your own writing, or type out and print copies for you to have readily visible for you to see in strategic places in your home, office, or car. It's amazing what just a few minutes a couple times a day can do when you "speak with the voice of authority—when you use your voice, release your authority and transform your life!"

Psalm 1

I am blessed. I walk not in the counsel of the ungodly. I do not stand in the path of sinners. I do not sit in the seat of the scornful. My delight is in the Word of the Lord, and in His Word I meditate day and night. I am like a tree planted by the rivers of water that brings forth its fruit in its season, whose leaf also shall not wither. And whatever I do prospers. All the time!

I Corinthians 13:4-8a

I endure long and I am patient and kind.

I am never envious nor do I ever boil over with jealousy.

I am not boastful or vainglorious. I do not display myself haughtily.

I am not conceited, arrogant or inflated with pride. I am not rude or unmannerly.

I do not act unbecomingly. I do not insist on my own rights nor my own ways.

I am not self-seeking. I am not touchy, fretful or resentful.

I take no account of the evil done to me and I pay no attention to a suffered wrong.

I do not rejoice at injustice or unrighteousness. I rejoice when right and truth prevails.

I bear up under anything and everything that comes.

I am ever ready to and I do believe the best of every person.

My hopes and expectations in Christ are fadeless under all circumstances.

I endure everything without weakening.

I never fail, I never fade out or become obsolete or come to an end. Never!

Psalm 91

I dwell in the secret place of the Most High, I abide under the shadow of the Almighty.

I say of You, Lord, You're my refuge, my fortress, my God. In You will I trust.

Surely You deliver me from the snare of the fowler and from the noisome pestilence.

You cover me with Your feathers and under Your wings do I trust.

Your truth is my shield and buckler.

I am not afraid for the terror by night, nor for the arrow that flies by day, nor for the pestilence that walks in darkness, nor for the destruction that wastes at noonday.

A thousand shall fall at my side, ten thousand at my right hand but it shall not come near me.

Only with my eyes shall I see and behold the reward of the wicked.

Because I have made You, Lord, which is my refuge, even the Most High my habitation, there shall no evil befall me, neither shall any plague come near my dwelling.

For You have given Your angels charge over me, and my angels keep me in all my ways.

My angels bear me up in their hands, lest I dash my foot against a stone.

I tread upon the lion and adder, the young lion and the dragon do I trample under my feet.

Because I have set my love upon You, therefore You deliver me.

You set me on high because I have known and I know Your name.

I call upon You and You answer me. You're with me in trouble.

You deliver me and You honor me.

With long life You satisfy me and You show me Your salvation. Always!

As a closing thought, I want to leave you with this: An end result of this boldness of speech that releases authoritative and dominating words is "To lift up those that are oppressed and cast down, to bring deliverance to the captives and salvation and light to those drenched in sin and darkness." In the Amplified Bible, Job 22:29-30 says, "When you are cast down and humbled, you will speak with confidence, and the humble person He will lift up and save. He will even rescue the one (for whom you intercede) who is not innocent; and he will be rescued through the cleanness of your hands."

For all of the great promises that God has given us, there is always an ultimate purpose behind these promises, and it's not meant to stop with just ourselves. Our authority and the fulfillment of all God's promises to us are given to us to be generously given to others. We get to personally experience the enjoyment and fulfillment, the very benefits of these promises, but God's intent is that we pass them on. So to whatever degree the words and teachings in this book have impacted you in a positive and valuable way, pass it on.

Grow in using your voice, in using your words, with authority directed to you from the heart of God. Use your voice, release your authority and transform your life!

About The Author

Lance Ivey is a full time traveling minister and teacher to churches, bible schools, ministries and businesses across America.

Lance has served as Executive Director of Heartland School of Ministry and Christian Education Director at Heartland Family Church in Irving, TX. Lance was also Assistant Director and a full time-instructor at Victory Bible College while serving on the Pastoral Team at Victory Christian Center in Tulsa, OK.

Prior to this, Lance taught in Rhema Bible Church's Healing School and helped pioneer the men's basketball program at Rhema Bible College in Broken Arrow, OK, winning two bible college National Championships.

Lance Ivey Ministries
P.O. Box 1127
Roanoke, TX 76262
817-653-2084
www.lanceivey.com
lance@lanceivey.com
Search for the Lance Ivey Ministries App
in the Apple and Google App stores.

PRAYER OF SALVATION

God loves you—no matter who you are, no matter what your past. God loves you so much that He gave His one and only begotten Son for you. The Bible tells us that "...whoever believes in Him shall not perish but have eternal life" (John 3:16 NIV). Jesus laid down His life and rose again so that we could spend eternity with Him in heaven and experience His absolute best on earth. If you would like to receive Jesus into your life, say the following prayer out loud and mean it from your heart.

Heavenly Father, I come to You admitting that I am a sinner. Right now, I choose to turn away from sin, and I ask You to cleanse me of all unrighteousness. I believe that Your Son, Jesus, died on the cross to take away my sins. I also believe that He rose again from the dead so that I might be forgiven of my sins and made righteous through faith in Him. I call upon the name of Jesus Christ to be the Savior and Lord of my life. Jesus, I choose to follow You and ask that You fill me with the power of the Holy Spirit. I declare that right now I am a child of God. I am free from sin and full of the righteousness of God. I am saved in Jesus' name. Amen.

If you prayed this prayer to receive Jesus Christ as your Savior for the first time, please contact us on the Web at **www.harrisonhouse.com** to receive a free book.

Or you may write to us at

Harrison House • P.O. Box 35035 • Tulsa, Oklahoma 74153

The Harrison House Vision

Proclaiming the truth and the power

Of the Gospel of Jesus Christ

With excellence;

Challenging Christians to

Live victoriously,

Grow spiritually,

Know God intimately.

About the Author

Emmanuel Ahia, PhD., JD, LPC, NCC.

Dr. Ahia is one of the pastors and the Director of Calvary's Christian Counseling Center at Calvary Full Gospel Church, Fairless Hills, Pennsylvania. He believes the Word of God is a complete and enough resource for bringing rest to those who are "weary and burdened" in spiritual, emotional, personal and professional problems and issues. He earned a BA and MA degrees from Wheaton College in Illinois and a PhD from Southern Illinois University. His JD degree is from the University of Arkansas School of Law. For over thirty five years he has been a clinician, counseling professor, and administrator in five Universities (Rider University, Johns Hopkins University, University of Arkansas, Central Michigan University, & Southern Illinois University). At present, he is a Professor and Director of the Ed.S. & MA in Clinical Mental Health Counseling Programs at Rider University. Dr. Ahia is also a practicing attorney and experienced in mediation, counseling supervision, healthcare law, and ethics. Over the years, he has presented papers in national and international professional conferences and is the author of many books and articles in counseling and mental health law, including Legal and Ethical Dictionary for Mental Health Professionals.

He has been married to his wife Ruth for over forty years. They are blessed with four children and six grandchildren, all of whom love the Lord.